The Rose with 7 Thorns

Disclaimer

This book is a memoir, reflecting the author's recollections of events over time. While the events described are based on the author's lived experiences, some names and identifying details of individual's have been changed to protect their privacy. In some instances, events and conversations have been condensed or recreated for clarity and narrative flow.

Copyright © 2025 Nichole Deweese (Nikki Milan)

All rights reserved. No part of this publication may be reproduced, distributed or transmitted in any form or by any means including photocopying, recording, or other electronic or mechanical methods, without prior written permission of the publisher, except in the case of brief quotations embodied in critical reviews and certain other noncommercial uses permitted by copyright law. For permission requests write to publisher, addressed "Attention publisher" at address below.

nichole.deweese@yahoo.com

Book written, edited & illustrated by; Nichole Deweese (Nikki Milan)

Prologue

It was in my darkest hours of anguish that I found my most strength. My cries would be heard, my tears would fall as I'd give up once more. It was while I buried my head in the carpet that I had become closer to God. It was then that he'd save me once again. And because I shouldn't be here. She is supposed to be here. She'd go on to take her very first breath, while I'd take my last. Yet I came back. For reasons unknown. Having been stabbed and with a cold barrel pressed against my forehead and a sharp click, yet nothing. Maybe it jammed but it happened one more time and nothing again. Maybe he didn't load it right. Or maybe it was God that said, nope, not this one.

I'd pierce my wrist over and over, only to watch my veins dance around, maybe I was doing it wrong. With a cord around my neck affixed to a curl bar hung in the hallway, I'd kick the chair, only to fall while the bar fell too and hit me in my head. I clearly needed something sturdier. Maybe I could just take a bunch of pills? Maybe, but it never worked for my mama, why try? Drink myself to death? That's it! No, just a slow death with a lot of tears and painful memories. Ran over twice and not a broken bone. It didn't matter whether I tried myself or someone else tried for me. I survived it all and why?

I'm just here for the pain. I endured it all. Mama numbed hers, I didn't get so lucky. Nope, but I came into this world with these gifts, only they're not gifts. Some of them like curses. Grandma said they came from her, she had them too. And she was Cherokee Indian so there's no telling what kind of spiritual rituals my ancestors had going on back in the day. Maybe that's where all this shit came from or maybe it came from God himself but I'm what people call, an empath and a sensitive. I can feel other people's feelings, their pain, their happiness too. I try not to be around too many people though because someone around me might drain me and make me feel weak. Plus I don't like crying around people and I'm sure someone in the room might have some sad, fucked up energy about them.

I can feel things like spiritual presences from time to time around me and if it's negative, I'll get real nauseous and my skin will crawl. It's a yucky feeling and I hate it. I used to see dead people. I don't anymore and thank God. But they whispered to me. I don't know what the hell they had to say, I couldn't understand them. I'd feel the trembling in the ground, my ears would start ringing and I'd lose my hearing just before they came, those Cali earthquakes that I hated so much. I could never tell if it was going to be "The big one." But the worst was the dreams because some of them were real.

They'd come true. Some, not all. But the important ones came true and I couldn't stop them from happening. I saw them all die, woke up to turn on the news and there they were 15,899 dead. I was there, in Japan. Not physically, but spiritually. I saw the chaos, I felt the fear of every last person that ran past me. The one dream that hasn't come true yet was the one where I was murdered. But there were many of those. I died in different ways each time. And they'd affect me in real life. Had a migraine for a week, after being shot in the temple and left for dead in one of my dreams. That whole week I cried from this migraine, I felt numbness in areas of my body and cold, very cold. It didn't matter how many blankets I put on, how many layers of clothing. Just cold.

They say you can die from heart break too, I don't know why I haven't as many times as I should have. So many broke my heart. People I really loved. I cried so hard my heart felt like it just hurt literally. Maybe it was more like a heavy ache. But it was there. My heart still hurts for people sometimes. Mainly the ones I can't see anymore. I'd get drunk and tell my stories, all real of course. They loved hearing me talk about my life. I had some pretty funny stories. They'd say, "you have to write a book." I heard it so much throughout the years. Clearly I needed an outlet for my memories, and even my fucked up thoughts. And even though I know for sure, therapy would do me some justice, I'm too afraid they'd commit me to Norwalk. So, I'll just use you all to let it out and for free.

There you are. Now you have a role in my life. An important one. Because you're going to take this journey with me while I relive my memories. I cried real tears while typing this but I don't want your sympathy. I just want whoever is reading this to know that they can and will get through the tough times just like I did. I hope to be an inspiration. Bear with me, I'm full of shenanigans, and my life was full of adventures, some weird shit and fun times with the ones I love and because they're all dead, I don't know how much more time God will afford me to be here. So, here's my legacy and theirs too. Enjoy...

Dedications

All praises to the most high. Thank you God, for every second of breath you give me. For getting me through the hardest moments of my life. For never leaving my side and loving me unconditionally.

My grandmother Anna, may she rest peacefully. Thank you for giving us a home and a normal childhood, what was left of it. You were my grandmother but you were also my secondary mother and my best friend. I always admired your strength and looked up to you. I haven't forgotten about that dance you owe me. I love you my sunshine, to the moon and back.

My Nana, may she rest peacefully. You'd be proud of me for doing this. I miss all our coffee dates and the stories you'd tell me about your life. I look forward to many more one day, till we meet again. I miss you dearly.

My mother Julie, may she also rest peacefully. Mom, we had many ups and downs. None that we couldn't get through together. I never expected perfection from you. I loved you just the way you were. I knew you were unhappy. I just wanted you to love yourself more, ya know, the way your kids and grandkids loved you. I know that you knew you were dying and just couldn't bring yourself to tell us. I understand how hard that must've been. How do you say goodbye when you're not ready and without tears filling your eyes? You were the love of my life despite our many woes. I love and miss you incredibly.

My brother Michael, may you finally be at peace. Mom's death killed you in so many ways, you were so troubled and unhappy. I wish there was more I could've done because my words just weren't enough to heal your sadness. You were the best uncle, the best father and best brother. I'm glad you got the son you wanted for so long. You had a chance to experience fatherhood. We were supposed to grow old together, remember? We talked about it. How you'd kick my walker and make me fall and how I'd roll you down the stairs in your wheelchair. I think you were more than my brother, maybe you were my twin flame. That makes more sense to me. If I could've traded places with your fate. I would've. You had the biggest heart in the world. You were very special to each and every person you crossed paths with. You meant something to the world.

My brother Wayne, may you rest peacefully too. Fun loving and happy go lucky, I never met anyone in my lifetime as free spirited as you. Your sense of humor was unmatched. I used to wonder why you chose to live your life the way you did. Why you chose to leave the good life to struggle with us. After you passed away, it dawned on me that you didn't care about the great life you once had. What you cared about was being with your siblings, even if that meant you'd struggle. How unselfish of you. Did you feel guilty for having a better life? I sure hope not. We don't choose our destiny but I hear you choose your family before being born and if so, thanks for choosing us.

My brothers, thank you for all the wonderful memories, the laughs and the love. We were all we had for a while there. I could've never imagined life without you two in it, I still can't. I will always miss us.

To my baby brother, we've lost so much, this is a shared pain. But there is a reason we are the last two standing. For every important moment in your life, I will be there. Your wedding day, I look forward to that. Be the very best version of yourself always. I believe in you as much as I believe in myself. On the days where it's hard to hold your head up and on the days when you feel guilty to be breathing, you get up anyway and own this thing we call life. Because as hard as it is, we must give ourselves permission to live. And even on days where we don't always see eye to eye, know that your big sister loves you still.

To my nieces and nephews, thank you for keeping me on my toes. More importantly thank you for being so amazing. Even in your youth you understood that even adults need hugs and reassurance from time to time. To my children, all the "I love you's" and "Can I help you with anything's?" never went unnoticed. I'm so lucky to have such incredible children. I don't know where I'd be without you. I love you so much my babies. You are mommy's greatest masterpieces and the very reason I strive to be my best.

To my friend Crystal, thank you for always being there for me. Through both the smiles and the tears. If I ever needed a loan, food for the kids, advice or just an ear to vent to, you were always there without judgement. To all the people that took advantage of my vulnerability during my time of grief, the people that deliberately took advantage of my kindness for personal gain. To those failed relationships and friendships, thank you. It made me stronger and wiser. You showed me that nothing exposes character more than the way you treat people you don't think you need.

Chapter 1

Who would've known life would come with so many twists and turns? I could've never been prepared for what life would have in store for me. Born and raised in East/North Long Beach. My friends call me Stormy, my family, they call me Cole or Coco (short for Nichole). But my mama? Her favorite name for me was Bitch. It bothered me but I think it bothered my brother more. I'd often see his face turned up in disgust whenever she'd refer to me that way in front of him. Even though, my mama was a beautiful woman with a heart of gold. She just chose the wrong path early in life.

I'm an 80's baby and everyone knows that was the speed and crack era. I mean, that was when the shit really hit the scene. And anybody who was anybody was doing it. My mother wasn't exempt, nor was she exempt from the hooking scene. In fact I learned my mother started off using acid at 14 years old to numb her pain and started taking trips to the bay to sell her body. When I think back to my childhood, I don't remember much of it before the age of 7. They say your mind can block out all the bad memories, that's funny, it seems to be all mine wants to remember. And so here I am at 44 still trying to heal from the shit.

Nights were the worst, as my brother's sleep sound and peaceful in their bed, I'm awake as usual, 7 years old with sleep issues. And so, I just lay there listening to the loud thuds against the wall. Not really knowing what it was, I wondered, and I was curious enough one night to go find out. And so, I get out of bed and in the dark, I walk over to the door. I cracked the door just enough to peer in and see nothing at first but then I squinted my eyes and there, just in the corner I see something moving back and forth. Trying to focus my eyes so I can make out what it is, I realize it's my mama. Crouched down in the corner, knees to chest, just rocking back and forth and with each backward thrust her head hits the wall. Out loud I say, "mama?" She stops, head turns, eyes peering at me in the dark. She slowly gets up and then, like a bull, she charges at me, showing her black teeth. Scared, I'd slam the door shut, then BOOM, her head hits the door. This would come to happen often, almost nightly even. I feared my mother. Moments like that would go on to traumatize me for years to come but we'll get into that later. In the daytime you'd see holes in the wall. Some from mama's head, some from mine. I never let her come near my brother's when she was mad. I'd stand in front of them so she wouldn't touch them.

  On a good day you could catch me in front of a 24" tube t.v. dancing to Janet and Whitney's videos. "Rhythm Nati0n" and "I wanna dance with somebody" were two of my favorites and I knew every move, every step. You couldn't tell me nothing. In the mornings I'd walk my brother Michael to school and then come home to be with my little brother Wayne and my mom, on days when she was actually home. I'd usually find her slumped over the toilet vomiting. I'd put a cold rag on her head and rub her back because in my childlike mind, I had this idea that I could fix her. Sometimes mom would lock herself away in her room but other times she'd be gone and for days at a time we'd be alone with no food, she'd leave us there to starve on many occasion and with no adult supervision.

But those were some of the best moments for us, because me and my brothers would run the streets and do what we wanted. Me and Michael would leave Wayne home sometimes while we'd go steal from the corner liquor store. I'd run out with bread and milk while Michael would kick the arcade machine and steal all the quarters that would come out. We were quite the team, we always made shit happen. But I know that little Asian man hated us, I'm sure of it. Sometimes you'd find me and my brother's over at Jackson Park just next door with sheets trying to make tents between the bushes or sliding off the green water tanks. Sometimes we'd climb down and walk around the storm channel, we found a real human leg down there one time.

On some days we'd play on the railroad tracks, lay across the railroad until the train got close enough, then we'd jump up and run down the side of the hill laughing. In fact, I believe we were the reason they put the cement walls up along the sides of the tracks that are up now, to this day. We had no sense at all. Just kids with no friends and no toys, only each other to play with. So, we just made the best of it but it's those memories that I treasure the most, the three of us just enjoying what life we had, in that moment, together.

Some days mom and her boyfriend would take us dumpster diving behind the goodwill, they'd toss me and Michael in and we'd throw the clothes out. That's where our clothes came from, and I can assure you that those torn and stained clothes were most likely the reason we didn't have any friend's. The kids at school didn't like us, we were ragged and so they didn't want to play with us. My teacher Mrs. Davis, that grumpy old lady never liked me, she picked on me. And just like the kids, she teased me too. She treated me as if I wasn't worthy of an education because I didn't look the part of someone that needed one. She's the reason I hated school and rarely went. My brother Michael was being bullied by two boys that lived in the Carmelitos. I threw rocks at them and chased them home one day. They never messed with him again.

We spent many of our days next door at the park but on one day, we heard sirens coming down our street, in fact it was an ambulance pulling up in front of where we lived. Upon seeing that we ran home to find mama being put into the back of the ambulance. Head busted wide open, blood everywhere. As an 8-year-old girl, seeing something like that made me think my mama was dying. Her boyfriend beat her up again and there I am just crying and feeling bad for not being there to protect her. As she was being rolled into the back of the ambulance, she yelled out to our neighbor to take care of her kids. But she didn't, I don't remember her coming over not once to check on us. We were alone for what felt like forever. Yet, we survived.

I didn't think I'd ever see my mama again. And as far as I was concerned, no one gave a rat's ass whether we lived or died in that house. I shouldn't have been surprised when these men with suits on came to the door hoping one of us would open it, but I knew, for whatever reason, I knew they were there to take us away and I was not about to let anyone separate me from my brother's. They were my life and all I had. So, I told my brothers to jump out the back window and run to the tunnel under the railroad tracks behind the park and that I'd meet them there. I followed shortly behind and because I was unsure that it was safe to go home that day, I went alone back to the house to get a blanket and we slept under the tunnel that night, right under the railroad tracks. And that night for some reason, it rained, it rained hard that night. I remember watching it for a while before I fell asleep.

Now, you might wonder where our fathers were. Well, they just weren't around. We all had different father's, which I did not know at that time. My brother's knew theirs. I never met mine. I heard he left before I was born. He was someone that was said to have sexual sadism disorder and that I'd come to be conceived during an act of sexualized torture. Let's just say, I wasn't no love child, that's for sure. He used my mother, knocked her up and bounced out of fear that his girlfriend who was also pregnant, would find out.

Because after all, her and my mother were friends. From what I heard, my mama was head over heels for his sorry ass. My mama didn't know what love was, surely inflicting pain on her wasn't love. Yet she'd come to live her entire life thinking that being taken advantage of and being manipulated was a form of love. But she was being abused and she'd continue using substances to numb herself from the pain of it, and it all started with him. What a legacy to carry on, I admit, I'm ashamed to have ever been born as a result of it. But to be honest I guess I'd be ashamed if I were born a product of rape too, I mean because there were rumors about the Hispanic man raping my mother and him being my father and no one even knows who the hell he is. "Hey, Julio? Carlos? Whatever the fuck your name is, now might be the time to pop out and say "Hola." Because I have some damn questions. I just don't even want to fathom that either to be honest. Should I be glad to be here?

However, while pregnant my mama would come to meet my brother's dad, he decided that he would be my dad and even give me his last name. His heart was in the right place. He was the only father I knew. He stuck around for a while after my brother was born. Then he moved away, to the east coast. My mother had my second brother at some point and struggled with all 3 of us and with her addiction at the same time. She had food stamps that she sold for drugs to keep up with her habit. I remember not having food and seeing only bread on top of the refrigerator to eat, picking the green mold off of it and rolling the bread into a ball and giving some to my brother's. I don't know why mine always had a piece of hair in it, what an odd detail to remember.

I also remember finding a bag of nestle morsels in the very top cabinet, it must've been there for years but we ate them. I remember sitting in cold water with my brothers, shivering and so cold my chest would tighten up. Taking a bath in cold water felt more like a punishment to me. But I suppose when there's no hot water or gas to heat the water, what choices do you have?

One day while walking around the corner to the store, I'd meet this older lady named Georgia. She lived in the apartments next to the store. She was walking her dog and was nice enough to let me pet it. She took a liking to me and would invite me over on occasion for a sandwich and juice. I told her about my mama and brother's. She'd send me home with extra sandwiches for them. I've always been quite the opportunist so I had at some point concocted this idea that I could get her to adopt me, and my brother's, then we could live with her. So, with that in mind, I would slowly introduce her to my brother's one at a time. Starting with Michael.

So, on one particular day Georgia wanted to take me somewhere in her car so I met up with her. We went to some big store where she bought me a big bucket of double bubble to share with my brother's. On the way back I asked her if I could swim in her pool and bring my brother. She agreed, so when I got back, I went to grab Michael. We got in her pool, but he didn't know how to swim so he almost drowned and Georgia had to jump in and save him. That freaked her out and we weren't allowed over there anymore, my plan went right out the window. I was so mad at him that day.

I asked mama to get help. But that would require rehab and her finding someone to take all three of her kids. We all got separated for a while. I went to live across the street with Grandma Juanita and uncle Keen. Which was mom's boyfriend's family. Every morning grandma Juanita had me get her coffee ready for her. And I'd watch her cook. Uncle Keen would be watching boxing in the living room, he'd make me sit with him and he'd tell me all about the fighters. I grew to really enjoy watching Holyfield, Hagler, Sugar Ray and Tyson get down in the ring. Just to name a few. Those were my favs though. I developed a real love for boxing. It wouldn't be long before Uncle Keen would introduce me to the music he liked. Kool Moe Dee. LL Cool J and Eazy- E, just to name a few. He handed me an Eazy-E cassette tape and said, "Now Cole, this is real music here, you take care of this tape and don't you let grandma hear you listening to this." I ended up memorizing the lyrics word for word and when grandma wasn't around unc would let me perform for him, where I was allowed to use curse words. He was so proud. Lol… Eventually I'd move to the east coast with dad (My brother's dad, to clear any confusion), my brother Wayne went to live with his grandma on his dad's side. Michael stayed with mama, then at grandma's but not before my mama would be caught trying to drown him in the tub twice.

I was 9 years old and while with dad in Jersey, I learned how to read. I remember spending many days in the room reading "Mouse on a motorcycle" and "Charlotte's web" I remember lying in bed at night watching all the colorful spots on the ceiling move around. Often, I thought about my mama and my brother's and missed them. I remember being forced to eat vegan food because my dad's girlfriend was vegetarian, she didn't season her food either and it was disgusting. She'd make cake and it would have pieces of plant sticking out of it. I didn't like her very much.

I remember going to the VFW with dad and he'd buy me chips and pop and had me sit at the table while he drank with his buddies. I enjoyed that. What I enjoyed more was walking the dog every morning to the bay. Her name was Sally. While on our walks to the bay, I'd see horseshoe crabs all over the Bayshore, everywhere and many were upside down. I'd flip them over and they'd scurry away, many were dead.

I'd walk over to aunt candy's after school over in Cape May, while dad worked at a printing company. And every day my aunt would make me a peanut butter and jelly sandwich and bean & bacon soup. It beat my stepmom's food any day. I'd play with my cousin's. One day it was snowing, I had never seen snow before. My cousins were a bit older than me and very influencing, so we climbed on top of the roof in the back of the apartments. They jumped off and landed in the snow. They urged me to jump and so when I did, I'd land on a piece of cement curb hidden by the snow, spraining my ankle. Sometimes my aunt would take me to her job with her. She worked at a bed & breakfast, Victorian style. Sparking my fascination. I've been in love with them ever since. Still hoping to buy one, one day.

My brother Michael ended up in a car accident while still out in Long Beach with mama and was hospitalized, I overheard the conversation my dad was having, and I just remember feeling scared, crying and a feeling of helplessness come over me. I wanted to go home and although there were some days that I really enjoyed myself living with dad, it just wasn't the same, and to be honest I didn't feel like my dad liked me. I needed to be with my siblings and my mother. And so, I ended up going back home. But during that transition my brother Michael was being sent to the east coast. So, like two passing ships in the night, we never saw each other. Not that I remember anyway. We were traded off just like that.

Mama ended up moving in with grandma and grandpa and so that's where we stayed. That first night back my mama wanted to tell me how much better she was and how she had gotten a job. She took me by my hand and said, "come on." We walked just up the street to the Kmart parking lot and just stopped. I remember looking at the big K while my mom boasted about what she would be doing at this job. As she spoke, I stared at her. I could see the pride in her face as she babbled on. And in that moment, I was proud too. While living with my grandparents gave me a sense of belonging and stability, I still missed my brother's and wondered if I'd see them again.

Grandpa taught me how to ride a bike while there. Every day I picked the honey suckle flowers off the fence, pulled the stem out and sucked the drop of honey at the end. I slept in my grandparent's bed every night and while lying there

I'd stare at grandma's porcelain Siamese cat collection on the side of the bed until I fell asleep. I still remember the smell of the covers. The wooden bowls grandma would make her dinner salad in. So many memories. After a while grandma and grandpa bought a house with more space so that we could all be together. That meant that I would have my brother's back.

Michael ended up coming back but we never got Wayne back. The story that was told was, his grandmother had my mother sign some papers that would enable her to make healthcare decisions for my brother. But what had happened was that under duress my mother signed her rights away unbeknownst to her. It wasn't fair to any of us but maybe it was what was best for him, he was given a better life than my mama could have provided. Nonetheless we missed our little weewee and his absence did affect us. We often felt jealous from time to time too, that he had more than us. Grandma would take us to see him on holidays or birthdays, she'd bring him gifts and it seemed like no matter what she picked out for him, he already had it. We'd see pictures of him on sailboats and on jet skis. But he was happy, and I guess that's what mattered.

As for me and Michael, living with our grandparents meant that we would now be able to celebrate holidays and so came our first Christmas so to speak. I was about 10 years old, Michael 8.

We had a real tree and presents. Grandma would give me and Michael the store ad and say, "now circle 5 things you want for Christmas." Granny would put together these stockings with tootsie roll penny banks, LifeSaver story books and she always put some sort of fruit inside, a banana or an orange. Me and Michael would sneak into grandma and grandpas' room, undue the tape at the ends of the presents, pull the gift out, look at it, then slide it back in and retape it.

They always kept a cabinet full of snacks in their room with lemon pies and snowball cupcakes. Me and my brother would take turns looking out for each other while we jacked the snacks. Besides our grandparents giving us holidays, they gave us a home and some pretty amazing memories. Grandpa and Michael would spend many days raking leaves together and fixing bikes out on the backyard patio. Grandpa was more like the father figure that Michael didn't have, yet desired so much. They were very close. As I was to my grandmother. I looked up to her and wanted to be just like her.

Me, Michael and our cousin Monique rode bikes with the neighborhood kids almost daily and had so much fun. We were like the 3 amigos. We were always together. That was back when we had to be in the house when those streetlights came on. We didn't have internet, cell phones, tablets, social media or YouTube. You either had a bike or skates and had old fashioned fun with your friends outside.

That was our childhood and while it may seem that mom wasn't around, she was, she stayed in the backhouse. I'd try to stay away from her as much as I could. It was during that time in my life that I felt like my mother didn't like me. She was always randomly screaming at me and trying to hit me, calling me a bitch out of nowhere while walking up on me and shoving me around. I never knew anybody in my lifetime that could use their breasts as weapons, but my mom would lunge those knockers at me, while biting her tongue with her fists balled up.

While recovering from her addiction for the most part, I knew about her indulging from time to time with meth. She took a liking to beer and became quite the lush. It didn't help that she worked at a bar and had one hell of a personality. My mom was beautiful, but she was also funny. They'd tip her well. So, she dipped off into alcoholism and it wouldn't be long before I'd follow suit. Now in my early teens I had a new responsibility, a new baby brother. I'd be at home caring for him while mom worked. His dad was in prison for a while but when he got out, it gave me more the ability to have my own life. And with that newfound freedom came my first crush.

Chapter 2

In the summertime I'd go over to the high school and swim at the Jordan pool. On the first day of opening I'd pay my $1 to get in. Just a flat chested 13-year-old girl with eyes that sat fixated on that grown ass lifeguard. His name was Ty, 19 years old, tall, smooth chocolate skin with muscles and thick lips. I had never had a boyfriend, never dated and was a virgin. To be honest, I was still playing with barbies at that time. I knew what I liked though. I just wanted to be near him and to touch his muscles. I was so mesmerized by his beauty.

So every day I'd pay my $1 to get into the pool and it became less and less about me wanting to swim and more about me just needing to see him. I'd watch him, swim past him trying to get his attention. I did everything but pretend I was drowning. And why didn't I think of that? I could have for sure gotten him to pick me up from out of the water and get him to put his lips on me. Foolish little girl. Smh Lol.

I knew I needed to do something, it became my mission to get his attention. Majority of the girls my age had titties already. I was amongst the smaller population that didn't. And I thought that would be just what I needed to catch his attention. So, I had this bright idea that I would stuff my bikini top with toilet paper. What I didn't know was, toilet paper shreds in water. I'd learn that the hard way. And so, I'd go back and forth to the bathroom around every 20-30 minutes to re stuff my bikini top.

To my surprise, all my efforts worked. I don't know whether it was because he caught me staring a few times or because I had these humongous tits. But whatever it was, it worked because one day he came down off that lifeguard chair, climbed in the water and swam right up to me. I can't remember what we talked about that day, but I can assure you that we were together every day thereafter. Spending our summer days with each other. We played in the pool together, swam together and after the pool closed, he walked me home every day. And because grandpa was always at a union hall meeting, grandma at the hospital working and mom doing God knows what, lord knows where, me and Ty always had the place to ourselves.

So, on the first day he came over I walked to the kitchen to get him a glass of water while he waited on the couch. But to my surprise, when I came out of the kitchen he was standing right there with my titty in his hand (the toilet paper) and I was utterly mortified. I stood there embarrassed and with tears in my eyes. He wrapped his arms around me, as if to sooth me. Only saying to me that he liked me the way I was and that I needn't do any of that. And thank God because I was going through a lot to make this man believe I had DD's.

Most days we'd sit on the couch making out. I'd climb on his lap and just suck on his bottom lip. When we weren't together, we were on the phone together. I'd take the phone from out of the living room, plug it up in my room and we'd talk all through the night. He'd sing "I'll make love to you" by Boys ll men, to me. One day, after coming from the pool we went to my house as usual but this time we went into my room, and while kissing he laid me across my bed, climbed in between my legs. He pulled his meat out and slid my bikini bottoms to the side and proceeded to grind on me.

Suddenly I felt something warm shoot down my thigh, scared as hell I jumped up and screamed. I looked down and there was white stuff on my leg. Not knowing what it was I took off running to the bathroom, where I'd lock myself in and cry about whatever was on my leg. He was at the door trying to explain to me. I had a whole sex ed class from behind the bathroom door that day.

We continued spending time together and although we never officially had sex, he was officially the first man I had fallen in love with. But our relationship would eventually come to an end when mom decided to move out of grandma's and move us back to the east side again. With the new school year approaching I wouldn't have time to see him. I would still be attending Hamilton in north Long Beach but I'd be catching the bus back and forth and had to be home directly after school. So, believe it or not, I broke things off with him.

Only weeks later while sitting in science class I'd overhear big titty Tisha behind me boasting about her new boyfriend Ty. How they were having sex and how much she liked him. I knew in my heart who she was talking about, and I just sat there in silence with a broken heart. I thought big titties didn't matter huh.

Fast forward one year later, while spending time with my cousins over on the next block from where I was living, me and Monique were being nosy as usual. Peering out the bedroom window, observing the boy next door and up a few flights of stairs. He always had girls coming in and out while his mom was at work. I mean, he was seeing so many different girls that there was a rumor going around that one of them was his cousin and he didn't even know. We got a good laugh out of that.

It wouldn't be long before I'd end up friends with the girl that lived in the back, and she knew everyone in the neighborhood. She'd introduce me, even to that 16-year boy next door that slept around so much. And for some reason we both took a liking to each other. We started dating. And although he was sexually active, he knew that at 14, I still wasn't. He never pressured me. In fact, it was my friend living in the back that would tell me how good sex felt and how I should try it. She talked about it so much, it ended up sparking my curiosity so much that I'd go to my boyfriend and tell him I was ready. Knowing I wasn't and had no idea what I was getting myself into. But I figure, who better to teach me than my boyfriend. He obviously had done it and knew how to.

And so, I went over there, and we dipped off into his mama's room where we'd have endless sex for hours. Yes, hours. Went over there in the afternoon and came out at night. Silly me, I thought that because he was my boyfriend, he would be gentle with me. Boy was I wrong, he was the exact opposite. Instead, he forced himself into me while I was dry, the whole time. What should've been a beautiful first time for me was a nightmare. He would grab the edge of the bed and shove himself inside me, I was in pain. I cried, laid there and took it because I thought that's what sex was supposed to be. And he kept going while kissing me every few minutes to make the situation more manageable for me.

By the time we came out of his mama's room, all his friends were there ready to play all-madden, I guess they let themselves in. But the way they looked at me as I headed out, they must've heard me whimpering from the next room and clearly, they looked as if they wanted to ask if I was ok. But I wasn't. I took that walk of shame home that night. I got in the shower immediately, only to find I had started my very first menstruation cycle.

My mom took a special interest in me that night as if she could somehow sense the dirty behavior I had indulged in. Low key hiding in the bathroom just bullshitting, my friend came over. When she walked in the bathroom with something to tell me. She told me that after I left my boyfriend's house, she went up there to sleep with him after I did. And should I be surprised? With her sexual history, I shouldn't have been. In a rage I remember grabbing her by her hair, us tussling and me storming over there, I slapped the shit out of him. It would be years before I'd have sex again. That pain coupled with the betrayal of it all really messed with me.

In fact, that experience played a part in me somewhat turning into a tomboy. I started ditching school, my brother Michael right beside me, but I wasn't a bad influence on him, not me. He made me take him with me or he'd tell on me. I started wearing baggy clothes, usually my homeboy's clothes, Smoking weed, beedies and drinking on the brick wall in the back alley, that's where we all kicked it at. And living on the eastside, you can always expect to hear gunshots but one time they sounded hella close though, so we all ran and me? Well, I ran right into the bullshit. While running into my apartment complex I was grabbed by the neck by some man, while some lady yelled "let her go, she's a kid."

He did and I ran to my door, my little brother was on the other side of it alone. So smart at only 3 years old he pushed the chair in front of the door, we locked it and hid under the bed for a while before running through the alley to nana's house. But our neighbor, you could hear her screaming as they ran-sacked her apartment looking for merch or money. Just earlier her husband was arrested so we knew that the whole thing was a set up. Luckily no one was hurt that day. There was always something happening, if you walked into the wrong store with the wrong team on your jacket or shirt and you were seen, you'd be made to turn that shit inside out.

On a good day you could hear a few neighbors playing some good tunes on their boom boxes, the guys out in the courtyard at a card table playing dominos together and drinking 8ball's of Old E, the ladies laughing and gossiping as usual. The kids chasing each other. Everyone knew and spoke to each other. Some family, others like family.

Chapter 3

Now back in North Long beach at grandma's again and nearing my 17th birthday I'd meet an interesting pair of characters, we'll call them Bam and Chaos just to protect their identities. You could always find bam leaning against the brick wall next to the apartments he stayed at, just standing there all hours of the day. I don't know, maybe he was selling shit, who knows. I can't call it, but he had a thing for me and anytime I'd walk by he'd holla at me. I wasn't diggin him though, so I kept it pushing. I started seeing another guy out there with him suddenly, he was lighter complected, about my height, he was about 21 years old. Looked like he could've been the 4th member of H-town. He was fine damnit. That was chaos and Yeah, I liked what I saw. He had my attention and apparently, I had his. So, one day while walking past, he spoke to me and that's all she wrote. We were hanging out together every day, even with his friend bam. He was always around, in fact, those two were inseparable.

I don't remember why but I stopped messing with chaos for a short period of time. I was quite the player in my younger days believe it or not. But I never just left a guy alone without good reason so I'm sure it was something but let's just say, he didn't take it lightly and neither did his friend bam.

So, I met this siciliano guy and when I thought, I was going to just deal with someone else, chaos got wind of it, and it was a problem. I don't know how they found out about my new boo, but they did, and their crazy asses were at my mama's door banging on it and trying to kick the door in while holding guns. Yelling, "we know he's in there, tell your little boyfriend to come outside." They were trying to scare him off and it worked. I never saw him after that.

Me and chaos got back together eventually. That lasted awhile until one day while hanging out in his apartment him and bam shared, he said he had to leave and wanted me to stay there and wait for him, but I had a bad feeling and told him that, but he still left, and I wasn't about to stay so I went home. In the middle of the night there was a banging at my door. It was bam, when I opened it, he was frantic and practically fell into my arms. Something bad had happened. Chaos was arrested, the story bam told me was that chaos went to his baby mama's house and walked in on her having sex and blew the guy's brains out. I didn't know what to think, I just know I cried, I didn't understand why he was even there, I was hurt and confused. Bam was crying too, and we just cried together that night.

Bam was at my house every day thereafter, and every day I asked him if he'd heard from chaos and if there was a way I could talk to him and every day he said he hadn't. That he didn't have an address for me to write him, he didn't know where he was at. He said that chaos had called him one time and said he loved me. Said that I should move on because he'd be in there for a while, that he was looking at a lot of time and for bam to look after to me if I needed anything. That upset me because I wanted to be there. I was willing to ride it out with him, whatever that meant. And I just knew Bam was lying to me.

As time continued to pass, bam was still checking on me daily, as if I had somehow taken chaos's place in his life. The truth is, we grieved for the loss of him for a long time because even though he was alive, he was gone from us, and it did affect us. But we were there for each other. I started drinking more during that time, it didn't help that mom was bringing home 40 ounces of beer. So one night mom mentioned playing quarters in the backhouse which is nothing more than a huge room with a bathroom built into it. Me and my mom shared that room. One side was the living room and the other side like our bedroom. I called my homeboy from across the street to come over, he did and brought his friend Ramirez. Right away, my first impression, for some reason I didn't like him, and he looked familiar too, but I couldn't place him.

As the night went on, we all played quarters, me not being very good I kept losing and having to take shots of beer. We were all pretty wasted, especially me. At some point Ramirez had a question for me, his question was, "why do you act like a stuck-up bitch when I try to speak to you on your way to school?" It then dawned on me who this guy was. Every morning I'd see him on my way to school, and every morning he'd try to converse with me from his car, while stroking his penis, asking me if I needed a ride. A fucking pervert, that's what he was. Sensing frustration and agitation in his voice and not knowing whether he was dangerous or not, I didn't want to anger him, so I replied with, "I'm sorry, I don't usually pay attention when I'm walking to school."

At some point I ended up hopping in the shower and I remember the water being so hot that I got out, wrapped a towel around me and laid on the floor because I felt like passing out. I do remember hearing my friend from across the street banging on the door trying to make sure I was ok. I must've been in there for a while. He managed to get into the bathroom, he'd pick me up and put me in bed and cover me up. But I'm scared of heights and the bed seemed so high, I kept climbing out of it and laying on the floor in front of the fridge because there was cold air coming from underneath and it felt good to me. My friend picked me up and put me to bed a few more times when I finally stayed in bed, I remember watching my mom, my friend and Ramirez continue to drink from across the room and eventually I fell asleep.

I had suddenly awoken to Ramirez not only on top of me but inside me. Still feeling out of it, the room spinning and feeling like vomiting I yelled over and over for him to get off of me. He never once reacted to my screams at him. He kept going. And I kept trying to push his big ass off of me. Now crying and feeling helpless, I look over and see my mom in her bed right next to me, facing me with her eyes closed. And all I wanted was her to wake up and help me. She never did, she slept through it, the entire time I was next to her being raped. The only thing I could do was close my eyes and pray it away. As Ramirez began to move faster, a strength came over me, a strength I never knew, as if it weren't even my own. I sat up and pushed him off me and onto the floor. He rushed out the back door. I climbed out of bed, stumbling I managed to lock it.

The next morning, still feeling wasted I called bam and as usual he was right there for me. He was irate after telling him what happened. He went across the street to ask my friend where this guy lived. My friend was already scared of bam, so he told him right away. We all went over there, it was literally right up the street. When we pulled up, we saw Ramirez and a few of his friends on the lawn. The friends on the lawn walked off when they saw bam walk up. Bam was fit and tall with nice buff arms, so he looked intimidating enough and he loved to fight.

So, I shouldn't have been surprised that he left Ramirez lying in a puddle of his own blood. Then he came over to the truck and pulled me out and made me stomp on his head, even yelling at me that I didn't do it hard enough. That I had to make him pay for what he did to me. And so, I did. Over and over. His eyes fixed open, I don't remember if he blinked. I felt like he was staring dead at me though. We left when he was motionless. I just know I never saw him again. His face continues to be imprinted into my mind even 25 years later.

After that I slept with a butcher knife under my pillow and oddly enough, one month later the same situation happened again. Only it was my mom inviting a friend of the family over. Leo was his name and he brought a friend with him, I had no idea my mom had brought anyone in because I was sleeping. I woke up to my mama screaming. Leo was on top of her, raping her. While this other cat was on top of me trying to take off my clothes. He didn't succeed. I reached under my pillow, grabbed my knife and stuck it to his neck. He got up and left. I grabbed Leo from behind and threatened to slice his neck up and he quickly took off too.

I never seen Leo again but I did see the friend he had brought over that was on top of me. He was hanging out across the street in front of some apartments across from Jordan high. I found out who he was, some cat not much older than me.

Maybe early 20's. I called some homies up and watched them pull up and pack his ass out for me.

With all the little bullshit going on at that time in my life and bam being there for me, through it all. Just like he told chaos he would, It wouldn't be long before mine and bam's friendship would turn into something more. We ended up dating for the next 2 years. We fell in love with each other. I got pregnant twice, he didn't know about the first time. I had my homegirl kick me in my stomach and make me miscarry. The second time I told him, it appeared that he was ignoring me. I'd page him and he wouldn't return my calls. I was alone and scared. I called up his mama and let her know I had scheduled an appointment for an abortion and to let him know.

She pleaded with me not to, as did my mama. But I just needed her to relay the message. The morning of the appointment, I left to have the procedure done. Upon my return, he was in the back house. I don't know how he got in, but he was angry. He asked me if I had done it. Upset, I threw the papers at him. He snatched me up by my neck, feet dangling, he proceeded to choke and yell at me "you killed my babies!" He let go and I had fallen to the floor crying. He had never put his hands on me before. After that, he dragged me up the street to his mama's house.

He showed me everything he had been hustling for, car seats, strollers, cribs, etc. Bam being a twin, assumed I would be having twins as well, he was right. According to him, that's why he had not been talking to me, because he was out hustling. And because he didn't want what he had bought to go to waste, he'd continue trying to get me pregnant again. He had become more possessive. Didn't like the clothes I was wearing and so he came over one day, went through my drawers, pulled out all my clothes, put them in the driveway and lit them on fire.

He brought me his mama's clothes to wear. He was making me go to church, he said I needed Jesus, yet he was a whole pimp with actual hoes. I never saw them, but I knew. If we walked down the street and a man looked at me, he'd hit him. He was crazy and getting worse, I ended up leaving him. Vowing to never deal with an Aries man again.

But that wouldn't be the last time I'd see Bam. In fact, me and a homegirl of mine went to get a hotel to bring in my birthday, it would be just me, her and a homeboy of mine that I had hooked her up with. The three of us bought some liquor, got the room and was big chillin. My homegirl wanted to get her groove on so I stepped out to give them privacy. I went downstairs to smoke a cigarette, when suddenly Bam walks up out of nowhere mad as fuck. Assuming I was at this hotel with another man. I'm trying to explain to this nut job that the only man there is the one my friend is sleeping with.

Suddenly a car pulls up in front of us and it's Thai. Thai is my homegirl's ex that she just ended things with. I'm confused as fuck as to why Bam and Thai are there and how they knew where we were. Come to find out, they both popped up at my mama's house looking for us. She told them exactly where we were. I had no idea why she would've done such a thing but some shit is about to go down because my friend is up there screwing another man and I have to make sure he doesn't get up there.

We didn't have cell phones back then and I had to warn her. They were both out there in my face, Thai wants to know where my homegirl is at and Bam thinks I'm hiding a man from him. They were loud and disruptive, I didn't want to get kicked out of my room so I took off running to the other side of the hotel. I was trying to get to the other staircase, but they were on my ass. I managed to get up there, I'm banging on the door for my homegirl to let me in and I'm telling her to get dressed and hide ol boy.

She's panicking, I'm panicking. Just then, both Bam and Thai are standing behind me. Through the door I told her he was behind me. She decided to open the door and come out to talk to him but they weren't going to let that fly. Both Bam and Thai pushed that door open and all you see is my homeboy scrambling to get his clothes on which he didn't manage to do. He darted out that door butt ass naked. And because Bam enjoyed fighting, he took off with Thai and they both chased my homeboy. Me and my homegirl were so scared for him, but he managed to get away. Now my homegirl and her ex are fighting, they ended up leaving. Now I'm stuck there with Bam, he wouldn't leave because he thought I was waiting on another man to show up so he stayed the night with me. That would be the last night we'd spend together.

I found out later that the story Bam told me about Chaos and why he went to prison was a lie. In fact, it was a confrontation at a gas station with another man. Bam made up this story so I would leave Chaos, leave him to rot behind bars so he could fuck on me. In fact, he testified against him. Lied to me about not knowing where he was. Chaos had been trying to reach me and Bam cock blocked the entire year. The streets were talking and Chaos got wind that me and Bam were together. I heard he was angry and rightfully so. And the whole time, I had no idea I'd end up with the snitch that helped convict my boyfriend that would have him behind bars for 25 to life.

Chapter 4

Within the next year and a half I had become quite an alcoholic. I blame my past. It made it acceptable, at least in my mind, it did. I was at home drinking one afternoon, when I had run out of Hennessy. My mom was at work, down at the bar. I knew for sure my aunt had liquor at her house, so I started walking from north Long Beach over to Compton. Cutting through the streets, taking a short cut I'd run into some cute guy while walking under the 91 freeway on Myrtle and I knew I shouldn't be walking down Myrtle because every time I did, something would happen.

Like the year before, while walking, a guy pulled up to me trying to get my number and upon me ignoring him, I heard a gun cock. I looked over and he was pointing a gun at me. I froze, he laughed and pulled off. But this guy was on foot, walking with another guy while stopping me in my tracks. He introduced himself only as Grimey. We had a small conversation and just so I didn't forget who he was, he wrote both his name and number across my forearm with a sharpie marker. Being both young and somewhat intoxicated, I thought it was cute. I laughed it off and continued my walk to my auntie's house.

I stayed over there for a bit, drank a little, hung out with my aunt and my cousin's. By the time I *began to head back it was starting to turn dark. It didn't take me long to get home but when I got there, I called Grimey, making sure to dial *67 first so that he didn't have my mama's landline number. We talked for a bit before he decided we should link up and hang out. The plan was to meet up where we had met earlier. And so, we did, he brought me a 40oz. of old E, I was already tipsy and didn't really want to drink anymore so when he wasn't looking, I was pouring some out on the grass, while we walked and talked. We didn't really have a destination. But we just wanted to hang out with each other. So, to me, I was cool with hanging out in the open.. Still wearing my skirt and flip flops from earlier, it started to rain out of nowhere, so we sought shelter over at Houghton Park.*

There we sat on a staircase on the side of the recreation bldg. We continued talking, laughing at times. He was good company. He told me that he didn't particularly like that park because something had happened there years ago. He started telling me the story. He said that he and a few of his buddy's went over there to hang out one night and there was a girl there with them. The following day they all had hung out, she had gone to the police and told them that they had pulled a train on her and raped her.

Obviously, hearing something like that made me feel a bit uneasy, but I shrugged it off. He didn't look like he would do anything like that, women lie about that kind of stuff all the time. As the rain started to die down, we started leaving the park. He wanted to hang out a little while longer, which I was okay with, but I was sure to let him know that my curfew was at midnight, even though I was 19 and hadn't really had one. We went by one of his friend's houses, he stayed just up the street, in a backhouse.

When we got there, I realized his friend was a guy I had gone to school with. That made me feel more comfortable. We sat on the couch, they passed blunts back and forth, I chose not to smoke that night, I was still tipsy. As I sat there, Grimey told me some other shit that I could not ignore, what he told me would change everything, the whole damn narrative. He mentioned to me that he had met me before, when I was 12 years old. At this point I'm looking at him crazy. He said he pulled up to me on a motorcycle and I ran. Oddly enough, I remembered that happening, only because the sound of motorcycles always startled me. He told me my address, the name of my little brother. I don't know how he knew these things and I was freaked out about it. I was ready to leave at that point. Feeling like, maybe I shouldn't be there. I'm not going to lie, I was low key scared.

He and his friend smoked and eventually nodded off. As it started inching more towards midnight, I started to leave when he raised his head up and asked me to stay a while longer. We went back and forth briefly, and I didn't know what he was capable of, seeing that he was nodding off, I figure I'd wait till he knocked out again just so I wouldn't have any issues with this guy.

He tried to kiss me a couple times, I pulled back. Eventually he ended up nodding off again. I started to creep out the door but as soon as I opened it, he woke up asking me where I was going. I sat back down. I just couldn't win, and I was starting to grow agitated. When he nodded off the third time, I actually got out the door that time and down the street. By then it was raining hard again. It is now after 1:00 a.m.

As I'm walking briskly down the side of the 91 freeway on 67th street, it's dark, there is little to no lighting, it's quite creepy to be honest. I was thinking about what he had said earlier and wondered, had he been stalking me all this time? As I got closer to the underpass, I heard yelling behind me. It was him, standing in the rain yelling "why would you leave me standing out here like this?" Confused because I didn't leave this man standing anywhere. I said, "I have to go home, I'll call you tomorrow." I turned away to continue walking, thinking he would go back to his friend's house. I didn't look behind me, not once, as if I needed to.

I made it under the freeway underpass, having shelter from the rain in almost total darkness, I decided to light a cigarette just to get a few puffs before heading back out into the rain. But before I could do that, I heard screaming from the top of the tunnel, echoing through the still of the night like something out of a scary movie. Quickly I looked back and saw him up there, he yelled, "don't you ever walk away from me like that." He charged down the hill after me. I literally ran out of my sandals, dropped my box of cigarettes and took off. This man was full fledge chasing me through the streets in the middle of the night. I was terrified, I didn't know what he was going to do to me.

Out of breath, I felt him behind me. I didn't need to look, I just knew he was there. My dumb ass slid across somebody's wet grass. I got up pretty quickly and felt him grab the back of my shirt. I struggled to get loose for a minute, not giving a smooth fuck whether my shirt tore or not. I was just trying to get away. I found a truck parked in a driveway and hid behind it. Trying to be quiet and catch my breath at the same time. I didn't hear anything for a while, and I felt like I was back there for a long time. But suddenly, under the truck I saw his shoes. He was standing right there. I wasn't sure if he knew I was behind there, but my heart was jumping out of my chest.

It was at that moment that I had to decide whether I'd stay put or take off running. Either way was a risk. I stay behind the truck, he comes behind there and snatches me up. I run out, he grabs me. I didn't know what to do until I felt like I didn't have a choice. I just took off running. Never once looking behind me. I continued to zig zag through the streets and at some point running through the alley, which wasn't a very bright decision.

I wasn't really thinking clearly at the time. I finally made it to the gate of the back house. I struggled to get it open. Couldn't find the key then just couldn't get it open. I think I dropped the keys at some point too. Eventually I got the gate open and when I did, I quickly locked it behind me. I sat on my bed and just started crying. My mom woke up and asked me what was wrong, and I told her. She sat up in her bed, clearly concerned. It was right then that I heard him yelling my name outside the house. I froze with fear. My mom was pretty freaked out too.

The following morning, he called my mom's house phone and when I answered he said to me, "I hope I didn't scare you." I slammed the phone down. I don't even know how he got her number. My mom would go on to change her number a few times, each time he'd get it somehow. The calls continued. I was paranoid about leaving the house.

It wouldn't be long before I'd end up moving back to the east coast. With my Greyhound ticket, I contacted the homie to front me with some shit to take with me to get off down there. This was before 9/11, were talking "99" and trust me when I say we were getting away with some shit for sure. With my cousin and my brother in tow right along with me, we made that 3-day trip.

At some point passing through Tennessee, we glared out the window, checking out the massive acres of land. I'll never forget the look on my cousin's face when we drove past some wooden posts along the side of the road with nooses hanging from them. She's mixed and so it was a grim reminder for her that racism indeed still existed in other parts of the world. In Cali, you wouldn't see any of that, not where we're from.

But in that moment, I wished I could've taken that vision from her. Make it all go away, as if it hadn't happened. But it did, it was indeed real. More importantly it was real for her. It was a part of her history. As she sat there, I watched tears roll down her cheeks. I put my arms around her, and we cried together. She was more like a sister to me and I couldn't protect her from that pain. From what she may come to experience in her lifetime or what she might see. It hurt me because it hurt her.

None the less our journey continued. Finally arriving in Atlantic city. While out there I had a handful of jobs all at once. One thing I always knew how to do was keep busy. And I enjoyed making money. I met a girl named Andrea, and we became best friends, even going so far as to getting matching tattoos so we'd never forget each other. She had come down from Florida for the summer with her sister. They had come for the summer jobs. It seemed like there were a lot of people there just to work.

And it turns out, there was some racism I'd come to encounter while there. One day while walking to one of my job's, a place called the Wawa, some white boys on bikes decided to throw glass ornaments at me. All while yelling at me and calling me a wop and a N lover. Of course being from Long Beach, growing up in an urban neighborhood and going through some shit, one thing I had was heart. So for whatever ornaments that landed on the grass and didn't shatter, I chased them assholes on foot, lodging them shits at their heads and all because, I'm not no punk bitch. They had that coming.

Drama wouldn't end there, I started to have issues where I was staying. There were inappropriate things that occurred and when I raised awareness about it. I was treated with disrespect and put out on the streets. With nowhere to go I slept in the park with all my shit like a bum. The night before my flight I needed a ride to downtown Philly. I asked my dad for a ride, only to be told no again. I went to ask the neighbors and they ended up taking me, my flight was early in the morning and I needed to be nearby. We went to the airport, I picked up my standby ticket and was dropped off at a motel in downtown Philly.

I had just enough to get a room with not a cent left to my name. I was starving, there was no doorknob on the door in my room, I stacked chairs up in front of the door so no one would come in. There were men outside my room talking and laughing all night. I never slept, I was scared and I don't know how many times I packed and unpacked my stuff throughout the night. But it was enough times to keep me awake.

Around 6 a.m. I heard some sort of commotion outside. There were people down there putting their luggage in a van. I could only assume they were headed to the airport. Now I have been racking my brain all night trying to figure out how I would get to the airport in the morning. I figured, since that's where they were headed, maybe they could give me a ride. I spoke with the driver, explained to him that I didn't have any money I could give him but that I needed a ride. He said to me that he is there to give everyone a ride to the airport free of charge and that if I don't hurry, I'll have to wait on another shuttle later. So of course, I ran upstairs to get my shit. Returning my key to the front office, which I didn't need anyway because there was no doorknob, she gave me $5 back.

I thought to myself, "thank God, maybe I could buy something to eat at the airport seeing as I was starving. I made it to the airport. I bought a muffin and some water, it was all I could afford but it held me over until I got to Cali. I boarded my flight and sat tight for an 8-hour trip home. I'm not fond of high places, least of all a plane. So, when the plane got over Vegas, it hit a bit of turbulence and I just knew I was going to die. The plane was falling from the sky, and I was so close to home, I had almost made it. I panicked and I cried while staring out that window. It took a few people to calm me down.

Now with me being home, I'd have to deal with a very familiar dilemma that with all the chaos that had gone on in my time away, would make me completely forget about. So, within the first few days home, Grimey would start calling again. My mama answered it the first time, telling him that I didn't live there anymore, the same thing she had told him the entire time I was gone. And in his response, he called her a lying ass bitch and proceeded to tell her that he had just seen me at the store. My mama used to tell me while I was away, about his phone calls. Eventually they stopped, and I guess for us it was out of sight, out of mind.

I thought it would be a good idea to enroll in a school for nursing, I always wanted to be like my grandma. I moved temporarily, a quick fix to not be seen by Grimey. I went and graduated. It was one of the best decisions I had made. I moved back to grandma's house. I started working and buying furniture with each check and putting everything in grandma's garage, so that I could move and get my own place. There was nothing more I wanted than to have my own.

I met a man named Rome that would get me there quicker. He would sit outside of Atlantic Farms market, slanging. I chopped it up with him on a few occasions and he put me on. I made extra money on the side doing that for a while. I also had this girl I had met, some years younger than me, in her late teens. She was naïve and fast as hell. Easy target. I needed money and was willing to do what I needed, to get it. So, she would hang out with me outside of Atlantic farms and because she was beautiful, guys would hit on her often. I was sure to tell her, don't talk to any of these men before talking to me about it because I knew them all.

At least, that's what I had her believe. Some would ask me what was up with my homegirl and my response was always, you got to pay to play and she aint gonna give you no play unless I tell her to. So, you know what happened after that, I started making money off the Lil bitch and she didn't even know it. I needed the money so she was going to need to get it for me. One day while talking to her brother, he told me a story of what happened to his mother. Come to find out, she was murdered and found disembodied, chopped in pieces. She was a prostitute. That shit freaked me out. I stopped seeing her. I didn't want anything like that to happen to that girl.

Chapter 5

I met a man I was low key interested in. His name was Tragic. He pulled up to me in his car, I was attracted to him immediately. We exchanged numbers and would go on to speak with each other daily. I introduced him to family and oddly enough upon seeing my stepdad, I witnessed a little reunion. Come to find out they were locked up together. He actually asked my stepdad to hook him up with me but I was in another relationship at that time. What a coincidence. He lived close by, which made him very accessible. So, we spent time together regularly. One day we walked up to the liquor store and got chased by a crackhead that I had sold baking soda to. We laughed about that all night. He thought I was absolutely out of my mind. And maybe he was right, but he liked it, I know that. As we got closer, we grew attached, he wanted me to have his baby. He talked about it a lot. And me? Well, I wasn't really interested in the idea. I was more focused on getting my own place and had every intention of partying when I did.

One day, I walked over to see Tragic when I witnessed an argument between him and some woman. I stayed back to survey the situation, when I saw her speed off in his car. Or was it his car? Come to find out, it was hers. That was his girlfriend that he had been with for the last couple years. I had no idea. I broke it off with him. I spent the duration of the night crying.

About 3 weeks later, I met another guy and we started to spend time together. Being childish and feeling bitter about what transpired between me and Tragic, after some time I ended up sleeping with that man. The first time we had sex the condom busted and for the life of me, I couldn't understand why. So while he was in the bathroom I rolled over to grab the condom wrapper, only to find it had tiny holes in it, too many to count. Upset? That wasn't the word, more like pissed. We hung out still, for a while until he started to really show his ass and that was all I needed to see.

On my 20th birthday, I had every intention of getting wasted, when I found out that night that I was pregnant, most likely by my rebound. I had the chance to tell him one day while I was walking to work, when he pulled up to give me a ride. I hopped in and notified him of the positive test and he acted as if it wasn't a big deal, all he was concerned about was whether or not I was gonna give him coochie before dropping me off at work.

A week or two would roll by and Tragic ended up showing up at my grandmas to make amends I suppose. And we did, but not before I could let him know that I had slept with another man and that I was pregnant. He said that he would raise that child as his own, even if it wasn't his. For the next 5 *years, it was us. I remember many rainy days he would meet me halfway, to walk me home in the rain. Soaking wet. You couldn't tell me that man didn't love me. I'd call you a bold face lie. We ended up getting a place and moving in together. It wouldn't be long before he'd end up in prison.*

I was going through my pregnancy alone at that time. I didn't know what was happening to my body. I saw a commercial about prenatal care and it prompted me to go get a doctor. Around 6 months pregnant, a guy pulled up to me while I was walking from work, he asked for my number. I told him I was taken and obviously pregnant. He didn't like that so while I walked across the street, he sped up and ran me over. I saw him and jumped out of the way, luckily he just got my leg and nothing more.

I spent my days working and writing letters to Tragic and visiting every chance I had. Rain or shine, I made those trips and because I didn't have a car, I caught buses everywhere. For every holiday we missed together, I bought things and put them in a cabinet for him, clothes, shoes, all sorts of stuff. I'm just sentimental like that I suppose. We spent 9 months away from each other. My love grew more and more with each passing day.

At some point he was sent up north, where he'd do out the duration of his bid. Unable to get up there to see him, his cellmate had a girl that lived in Long Beach that was coming out for a visit. She picked me up and I rode with her for that visit. It was an emotional one. When me and the girl left for the long trip home, I cried, I couldn't stop crying. I felt so empty. She said to me, "it's okay girl, we'll come back."

In the meantime, I had a little girl on the way, I was so tired of being pregnant and I had gained so much weight. I worked at the convalescent home for the entire 9 months of my pregnancy. At the end, I had trouble breathing, I had to sleep sitting up. My daughter was 2 weeks late. I went into the hospital, they tried to send me home and told me to call my doctor. I went into an empty room, laid down in a bed and told them to call my doctor. I wasn't leaving until I had that baby. My doctor came in at 1:00 p.m. and proceeded to induce my labor. I'd lay there for 11 hours having contractions without dilating. At midnight my water broke, and my daughter got scared and curled up under my rib cage. I was in extreme pain. It would be another 9 hours before they would do anything for me.

My cousin Monique stayed by my side the entire time. I almost broke her hand. She fell asleep with her head on the side of the bed. I snuck out of the bed and proceeded to the elevator to leave, with the pain I was having, I decided I wasn't going to do this. I had changed my mind, I wasn't having that baby. Security came up there and everything, trying to get me out the elevator, I dared them to put their hands on me. The doctor came back in and scheduled me for a c-section at 9:30 a.m. They gave me something to sleep and I passed out.

The next morning my mom was there, my grandmother, and my friend. My mom put on her gown and went in with me. Tragic called and stayed on the phone with mama so he could hear her first cry. Within 15min my daughter was born. But they had given me too much epidural medication, so much, I was numb from the neck down, it caused one of my lungs to collapse. I died on that table while struggling to breathe. I'm sure my mom didn't know what was happening.

They ushered her to take my daughter to the nursery. And I watched my mama leave the room while taking my last breaths. The vision of her holding her granddaughter and scurrying off to the nursery was the last thing I saw. I didn't see any white light, no loved ones reaching for me. I don't have a magical story to tell about the other side. Everything went black and I heard the footsteps of people running around me and yelling, "grab the crash cart."

I woke up in another room, my family was at bedside. My daughter was there but I couldn't hold her. I was literally paralyzed from the neck down. I started regaining feeling a few days later, that's when I felt all the pain, my bruised and fractured ribs hurt the worst. When they resuscitated me, they injured them. It hurt to breathe, to cough, to slightly move or do just about anything else. I was in the hospital for 3 weeks as opposed to the 3 days I was supposed to be there. A physical therapist was helping me to walk again.

I finally went home, and within a week or two I noticed something was wrong with my daughter. One night she was burning up, I rushed her to the hospital, they kept her, fearing she may have meningitis, which was deadly. She was hospitalized for 2 weeks. She had cords all over her. I slept there every night, I never left her. I hadn't showered or really ate, barely slept. My mama and my aunt came up there and my aunt made me go to her house to shower, eat and sleep while they stayed up there with my daughter.

She had a bacterial infection and because I got her up there quickly, they were able to catch it before it spread. She could've died and almost did. After a series of antibiotics, I was able to take her home. The next 3 years would be a struggle because as she slept, not only would she snore like a grown man but she'd stop breathing. Something was wrong with her, I just didn't know what. I stayed up at night watching her breath and would nudge her every time she'd stop.

She choked on her food often. Doing the Heimlich maneuver became a daily routine. She was constantly on antibiotics for throat infections. They had her on asthma medications. By the time she turned 3 years old, I took her to a specialist that determined her tonsils were touching, almost completely blocking her airway. She was rushed into emergency surgery. The doctor was astonished and said to me, "I don't know how you've kept her alive all this time. I simply replied, "I'm a mom."

But at that time I was sleep deprived and working overtime at least a few times a week. Yet I was still struggling. I hadn't gotten my check yet but I needed to do laundry, I managed to come up on some quarters I found in my kitchen drawer. Enough for the dryer. So after work I decided I'd handwash my underwear at least and throw them in the dryer. I put all my handwashed underwear in there except the one I had on.

Came back out maybe 20 min later and I couldn't find them. Mind you, I'm sleep deprived so I thought I was hallucinating. I looked in the other dryers, washers, trash, everywhere. My underwear was gone but where did they go? It's midnight, no one could have mistakenly taken them, no one was doing laundry that late. Confused as hell, I took off the pair I had on and handwashed them and threw them in the dryer, there was 10 min left on it. I turned off the lights in my apartment and sat at my door in the dark, facing the laundry room, waiting for something, anything. 40 min later, while nodding off in that chair, I saw some tall, heavyset man with black clothing and long hair walk out of the laundry room with my underwear dangling from his hand. I threw my screen door open and yelled at him, "where in the fuck are you going with my underwear?"

He acted as if he didn't hear me and kept walking. I followed him to the staircase at the back of the apartments, where he walked upstairs and into his unit. He's one of my neighbors. I had lived there for a year and had never seen him before. I noticed a camera above his door, I freaked out and ran back to my apartment. It occurred to me that this man may be embarrassed and most likely doesn't want to be exposed, what if he does something to me now so I won't tell?

I became scared, with no money for underwear, I went to work without any, until I got paid. I contacted my landlord and told her about it, she didn't believe me, said that the guy was sweet and doesn't bother anyone but she had a plan to not only get me compensation but to find out if he really did it, so she could evict him. So the plan was to use her p.o box so he doesn't know what unit I'm in, if he didn't already. Put a note in his mailbox saying, "I saw you take my underwear and if you don't send me a check to this p.o box, I will expose you and seek compensation legally."

A week went by when my landlord called me over to retrieve a check that came to her p.o box. With enough evidence to evict him, she did. Upon talking to the neighbors, they had underwear come up missing throughout the years also. What the hell was he doing with them? Wearing them? We dubbed him the "panty bandit.

Chapter 6

Tragic finally got out of prison. I made his favorite, tacos. I had his drink waiting for him. I figured he was visiting with family and friends and then he'd come home later. I waited at the table with his dinner ready. I waited and waited. I waited some more. And then I went to bed. It was like he was still locked up, the only difference is, I hadn't received a phone call. I was beyond hurt. I went over to his family's house at some point, they said they hadn't seen him. But his niece who was around maybe 7 at the time blurted out that he had left with Dayshia.

That was the one that he was with before me. I guess while he was locked up, they made amends, unbeknownst to me. My heart was shattered. A month later, he was at my door and I wouldn't let him in. I mean, eventually I did. He didn't offer any excuses, he told me the truth, which I already knew. We fought, argued, cried, yet I allowed him to stay. Who was I kidding, I loved that man. That would be the beginning of a whole lot of fuck shit for the next 5 years.

I broke up with that man so many times. We needed money, he couldn't keep a job for more than a day, he'd work with a temp agency here and there. The one thing he knew how to do was slang and so I bought him enough to get started, that money was supposed to go back into the household, but it never did. This man got a check for 1 days' worth of work, I didn't get paid until Friday and there was no food for our kids. I had to go to my mama's house for a care package she made for us, while he took his check and bought some earrings instead of putting food in the house. We broke up that day too. I had developed a good relationship with his baby mama, so even though we broke up, I kept his son with me.

One day my apartment got raided, it was like a swat team at my door with guns. They thrashed my house and took him to jail. The police called child protective services because the house was so messy. I had been working double shifts and my daughter was with my aunt everyday while I worked, we were rarely home. I got tired of cleaning after Tragic and his homeboys.

So, there were blunt wrappers, tobacco from the blunts all over the table, along with 40-ounce bottles and dishes piled up in the sink. I had every intention of cleaning that day, considering I was finally off. So, I know how it must've looked. My aunt and my cousins came over to help me clean and put food in the fridge in case they did come. My apartment manager threatened to evict me that day unless I put in a notice to move, so I did.

I moved into Tragic's family's house up in South central. When he got out, he joined me. The abuse was getting worse. We had a mutual friend that I had known since middle school, way before I had met Tragic but they knew each other too. They were in the garage hanging out. Tragic wanted a beer, so I asked our mutual friend if he wanted one too. He said yes, when I came out with the beers and handed them both to them, Tragic grabbed me by my hair and dragged me through the alley. Our mutual friend got him off me.

I moved out shortly after, got another apartment back on the east side. I planned it well, no one knew I was moving out, I had given the manager the deposit, had furniture being delivered over there and everything. But within the first few days, there was shooting outside my bedroom window. Me and my daughter were scared. So, among the many times Tragic had blown my phone up, I answered at some point and had him come over. I didn't have any friends during that time, least of all any homeboys that I could've had come over instead. He made me get rid of everyone. I couldn't get rid of Tragic though, not after that. One time I was combing my hair, he swore I was combing it for another man, so he came up behind me and cut a chunk of it off. Just under my ear.

I broke up with him one day and had my mom and her boyfriend change the locks. I went over to my aunt's house afterward to hang out. I was there for a while when my mom had called and said, "why did you have us change the locks if you were just going to let him come back?" I didn't know what she was talking about. She said she thought I was home, she called my house, and he answered the phone. Confused, I called my house phone, low and behold, Tragic answered my phone. We got into it, he said I'd better get home, or he was going to cut up my brand-new Italian leather couches.

I started to head home when my aunt stopped me. She told me that he was going to beat my ass when I got there and that the couches were materialistic, they can be replaced. She told me to call him and tell him that I had called the police and that he had best leave. Even though I didn't really call the police, it worked. He left. Me, my aunt and my cousin went over there after. They went in before me. I was scared of what I would see. I worked so hard for everything I had.

I heard them gasp and I knew it was bad. He had not only sliced up my sofas, but he broke all the dishes, the bathroom window was broken where he had entered my unit. My place was thrashed. He stayed away for a few days after that. Then one morning I woke up from my sleep with him on top of me with a gun to my head. He had broken into my house again. He said he had a dream I was cheating, and he was going to blow my head off. Then he pulled the trigger, and nothing. Maybe it jammed or It wasn't loaded. But he did it again on another occasion. He wanted to put fear in me.

I was terrified of him, and it was worse when I didn't comply, so, out of fear, I started to comply. I didn't know what else to do. I figure I could buy myself some time while I was mapping something out. He continued to have sex with me daily. One thing we did have, was great sex, several times a day. But I had started to develop hatred and so I started feeling nauseous when we had sex. My skin would crawl when he would touch me. And even though we had been together for 5 years at that time, I had started getting pregnant. Three times, two months in a row and I snuck and had 2 abortions.

On one occasion while working, I began having pain in my back and abdomen, I went down to the er. I was having a miscarriage and needed to call Tragic to pick me up because I was being discharged. He walked in drunk, the doctor told him what was going on, when the doctor walked out, he started screaming at me. Saying, "you probably killed this one too. You can have another man's child but not mine." I don't know how he knew about the abortions.

We both knew my daughter wasn't his, her dad found out where my mama lived. Left all his phone numbers on the back of his cd cover with his face on it, to give it to me. She was supposed to put to away for me, but it was left out. When Tragic went over to my mamas house, he saw it on the table. I guess there was such a strong resemblance, he knew who it was. Tragic played it off like it was ok with him that I allow him to be in her life. One day he made me call him and set arrangements to meet. I did and afterwards he beat me for it. I never made it to the meeting. I didn't reach out again due to fear that Tragic would not only do something to me but to him as well. He did something with the cd and contact info eventually. It was never seen again. There were so many times that he would look at my daughter, get angry and just hit me out of nowhere.

He came home drunk one night and hit me for no reason at all. He usually went to sleep on the couch butt naked when he was drunk. That night, when he did, I felt like because he was acting like a bitch, he should look like one too. So, I shaved his eyebrows, drew him new ones, put make up on him, painted his nails and took two shoelaces, tied them together at the ends and tied one end to his thumb toe and the other end around the head of his penis, I punched him in the throat. He jumped up. His meat pulled and I took off running to the bathroom.

I slammed and locked the door and while he pounded on it, my fat ass, still having some baby weight on me, tried to climb out that little ass bathroom window and got stuck. Next thing I know, he's outside the bathroom window trying to pull me out the other side. I thought for sure he was going to beat me, but he didn't that time. He just laughed, said I was crazy and that he deserved what I had done. I slept with one eye open after that, so to speak.

There were times that he treated me as if he really loved me. I was really sick one time, he laid next to me and put Vicks inside my nose, wiped it when it started draining and continued to do that over and over until I could finally breathe right. But we were barely getting along, I was miserable. There was no escaping this man. I change the locks, he breaks in and I wake up with him next to me. I take him to his family's house for whatever reason, wait for him to walk in and I'd take off, he'd jack his brother's car, catch up to me on the freeway, try to hit my car and attempt to run me off the freeway. God forbid he's driving my car one day with me in it, he'd swerve, almost hitting the median or other cars while screaming at me, "bitch, I'll kill us both." I'd walk outside to go to work, tires slashed, or the gas siphoned out.

At work I had a friend I could confide in, we'd not only talk at work but at home when I could get a moment away from Tragic. So, when Tragic said he was going to the store for a blunt, I jumped on the phone with my homegirl. Tired and fed up I asked her how I could murder him and get away with it. I wanted him dead. So, as I continued to flip open and close this pocketknife I had in my hand, I went over different scenarios with her. I didn't want to go to jail, I didn't want to be away from my daughter. Then my next question was, what if I lace his drinks with drugs and he tests dirty with his p.o. I could get away from him that way. He'd go to jail on a parole violation, and I could leave.

Suddenly the front screen flies open. Tragic hadn't left, he was next to the door listening the entire time. He grabbed that pocketknife from me and held it to my neck. Said to me, "you want me dead bitch?" I thought for sure he was gone kill me but he got up off of me and went to the room. It was only a matter of time before something bad would happen. I knew in my heart that if I didn't leave soon, I'd be dead. People were only aware to a certain extent to what was going on with us. Behind closed doors I faced difficulties not many could imagine. So, I decided I'd try to just leave him at the apartment since he didn't want to leave. And I'd go stay with my aunt for a little while. So, I did.

I was at the bar with my aunt one night. My aunt made it to her house first. I wasn't far behind. When I pulled into her driveway, I opened my driver door to vomit, that's when I saw Tragic out the corner of my eye. Next thing I know, I'm waking up in the room we used to sleep in at his family's house. I don't know if I passed out on my own or if he knocked me out, all I know is that this fool kidnapped me. He was still knocked out when I woke up, I looked around, trying to make sense of where I was. With my heart jumping out of my chest, I moved around like a quiet church mouse, looking for my car keys. And I found them in the front pocket of his jeans that were on the floor next to the mattress. I quietly and slowly got them out of his pocket. Looked for my pants and shoes in the dark. Crept down those stairs and outside where my car was parked in the front. I got in and hauled ass back to the eastside.

Eventually I'd have to head back home with no real remedy. I had always told this man that I didn't like the police and so therefore I didn't want them at my house. And that, should I ever have to resort to calling them behind the shit he was doing to me, that I wouldn't be one of those women that got back together with a man they put in jail. That if I had to call them, it would be over for good. And I meant every word. And so, I had at that point, I concluded that it would be the only way I could get away, if that happened.

My brother Michael ended up coming down from Jersey. He wasn't supposed to but he had got wind that my mom's boyfriend was beating on her and so he absconded, jumped parole, for that reason. He ended up at my house with me. I needed him there and even though he didn't know the full scope of what was happening between me and Tragic he did see him argue with me and not allow me to go anywhere or do things. And every time that happened, my brother would say, "why can't she go? Go ahead Cole, you can go." Tragic never said anything, never got into it with my bro or nothing.

He knew and respected that my brother would throw down for me if need be.

On one particular day, my situation changed drastically. Tragic and my brother came into the house with brand new, stolen air conditioners they had taken from a nearby hotel while they were installing them. And they brought them to my house. I was leaving for work in a rush because I was late. I had mixed up my days off. Thinking I was off, I wasn't, my boss called me to get to work. Tragic asked for a kiss as I was leaving, and I ignored him. While trying to start the car, I realized he had left me on E. I started to walk to work, strait down Pch heading to long beach Blvd. on foot. The metro had just dropped off a shit load of people so there were a lot of people at the light, when Tragic pulled up on my brother's bike, next to me. He was talking shit to me. I told him, "Don't do this right now, in front of all these people." He continued to antagonize me, and people kept staring at us. I was embarrassed.

He followed me up the street, rode the bike next to me as I walked. I was over it, I was over him and I was ready for this relationship to be over. So, when he started to get disrespectful, I'd return the disrespect. I knew he couldn't take what he was so used to dishing out to me. He proceeded to yell at me publicly. Saying, "You tired of me?" Well, your ass ain't left yet." So, I turned to him and said, "I see your ass ain't went back to your daddy's yet."

That's when he swung at me, my eye started to swell fast, he turned around on the bike and rode back home. I grabbed my face and proceeded to walk to work when a woman ran across the street and yelled out, "Don't let him do you like that, there's a phone booth right there."

She was right, there was. And in that moment, I decided that I was done, officially done. That after 5 years of this b.s. today would be the last. So, I walked over to the phone booth, dialed 9-1-1 and said," come get his ass." The first unit came, assessed me, I told them what happened, where he was, and they took off after him. They came back and said that upon them coming to the door, both him and my brother bolted, jumped out the windows and ran and that they couldn't find him. I'm sure both my brother and tragic thought the police were there about the a/c units. I assured them that Tragic would kill me eventually if they didn't find him. And because I was absolutely sure he would.

They put me in the backseat, and we headed over, another unit was already there searching as well. They found him hiding under a car in the alley. Cuffed him, put him in the back seat and left. The manager of the apartment came down and asked me to put in my notice, just like my old apartment manager. Deja vu. I called into my job and told them I wouldn't be there. My brother made it back to the house after the chaos, he had no idea what had transpired.

He said he would've handled it and I knew he would have but knowing my brother would most likely, eventually get arrested for absconding. My protection would be gone, I had to do things my way. He stayed there with me for my last 30 days at that apartment. When I got back to work after my 2 days off, I was fired. My boss said that I had too much going on in my life. Mentioned that my boyfriend was calling hourly to make sure I was at work and now this. She told me to come back when I got my shit together. Making $17/hr. back in 2004 was a lot of money so I was crushed about losing my job.

At the time Tragic had 2 parole officers so both stopped by my house. The one I had known and spoken to for years asked me why I hadn't told him what was going on and I just told him I thought things would get better. I didn't press charges or testify, the D.A automatically picked it up so him having people threaten me wouldn't change anything. Not one person that was talking that shit ever showed up at my house anyway. The parole officer had the courts give me an order of protection issued by the D.A for 3 years.

He violated every last thing on that list of shit he wasn't allowed to do. Didn't make me no never mind, all I needed was 30 days to get out of dodge and away from that man and with that parole violation, I'd get at least 6 months. My mama and my 2 brothers needed somewhere to go at the time, so they moved in with me for my last 30 days at that apartment. I sent my daughter to live with my aunt. Things were happening around there, and she didn't need to be there. Some men were trying to break in one night while we were there. I believe he sent them, not knowing my family would be there with me.

Chapter 7

I stepped into the strip game 2 years prior, to make ends meet and because I had lost my job. I'd head right back in it, full time. My brother ended up getting caught a couple weeks later and extradited back to Jersey for a 3-year bid. Me and my mom went to see him at Theo lacy before he left. My car caught fire on the freeway on the way home while I was driving, we lost power and had to coast it off the freeway until it slowed enough to pull the emergency brakes. Lost that car. In less than a month I lost everything I had worked so hard for.

Starting over was a bitch. Me and my daughter stayed with my aunt for a while. My mom got another place. Me and my daughter ended up with her. We spent a good few years there. I was dancing and making great money, I was paying all my mama's bills and so she never complained. I worked at a club just down the street from mom's. One night after getting off at 2 a.m. I was pulled over for my taillight being out. The officer gave me a fix it ticket. I went on about my business, only to be pulled over again by another officer on my mom's street. He blocked my driver door with his squad car and spoke to me with his window down. Asked me a series of questions like...Where was I going? Where had I worked at? After telling him, he suggested I get in the back of his squad car and give him a lap dance or I'd be arrested. I told him that I suggested he get the fuck out of my face with that bullshit or he'd have a lawsuit to fight. He copped an attitude and pulled off.

That same year, I was visiting with my boo thang down on the eastside. Normally I'd stay the night with him, for some reason that night I decided to go home. Got pulled over on Anaheim and Atlantic by a male cop that made me get out the car so he could frisk me (fondle me really) he grabbed me and felt me up in areas he wasn't supposed to, repeatedly. Afterwards I was told to go on my way. I cried on the way home, feeling I had been violated. About 2 weeks later I'd get a call from a detective. He said he was working on an investigation of an officer after reports were made that he had molested several women during routine traffic stops.

He had on record that I was pulled over one specific night by that officer and there was no citation on file for me. He wanted to know what happened that night. And because I knew that the police get away with everything, I was not about to be targeted so I declined to give any info about that night. Only saying that I don't recall.

I was very troubled at that time in my life, I took it all out on paper. I had always written poetry, it was medicine for my troubled heart and overactive mind. I found a sense of peace when I could be by *myself in the still of the night. I could clear my mind of my thoughts, talk to God, cry, whatever I needed to do when I was secluded, alone. And so, I'd leave in the middle of the night. Most of the time, you could catch me in San Pedro on the cliffs, at that park near sunken city. I used to love sitting on the benches in the dark, listening to the whales sing.*

But this one particular night, I decided to go to the east side, to this park my mom had taken us as children. We called it the water park because it had these small waterfalls and a tiny lake there. It was right off PCH, just past Junipero. I pulled up and just parked, it was just past 1 a.m. I pulled out my notebook and just started writing away. I had completed about 4 poems when I started to feel a little eerie. I decided to head back to moms. I was driving down PCH. There were no cars in sight, as it was really late but at some point, a car pulled next to me. Driving at the same pace.

I thought it was kind of weird, there's like 3 or 4 lanes and for some reason these people wanted to drive along the side of me. Out the corner of my eye, I saw something, some kind of movement. I look to my left, at this car and I noticed a woman and man in the front seats and a little boy in the backseat. His whole body facing forward, while his head turned completely, looking dead at me, watching me. And for some reason I turned my head to look at him, I noticed his face change, right before my eyes. It distorted on its own, that boy turned into something. It scared me so bad, I pulled over and just kept saying, "I rebuke you in the name of the lord." Repeatedly over and over. That image has never left my mind. I believe it was the devil himself.

Still dancing and trying to heal from Tragic and all the other bullshit I was enduring in between, I started going to Vegas 2 weeks out of every month, I'd get a room and stack, come back home and drop a few racks on my mama and she was Gucci. I had the money, but it took a while for me to get my mind right after what I had gone through. I was suicidal for a while. I had attempted to cut my wrists a couple times, not because I was missing Tragic or regretted leaving but more because I couldn't understand how you could love someone so much and them not love you the same way in return.

It took me a while to understand that this man may have been attracted to me, he may have enjoyed sleeping with me, he may have even loved me the way he thought love should be. But at the end of the day, what he also had with me was a home, my car to drive, a woman that loved him too much to leave and someone to control and that was enough to make this man ruin not just my spirit but ruin everything I worked so hard for, not once but twice. I lost 2 homes, 2 car's that of which he never put oil in and kept up and that I barely drove because he was dropping me off at work and taking them. The heads blew on both and remember the last one caught on fire. I lost a good paying job, and my sense of direction for a couple years after.

He found me eventually, he was friends with my other brother for years, and because he was also staying with my mama, it gave him a reason to come over and get a glimpse of me and my daughter. By then, I wasn't afraid of him, in fact, I was annoyed that my mother and brother allowed him to even come over there. His friends were telling me that he would make them sit in the car with him at the end of the block and just watch me for hours. It prompted me to get my shit back together and leave and so I guess, things really do happen for a reason.

My grandfather had passed away during that time and so me and my daughter went to stay with my grandmother for a while to look after her. I enrolled in UEI college, graduated with a 4.0 and obtained a license in dentistry. I was able to go back to work at the hospital, it had been 2 years and so it was about time I got back to my career and what I did best. My grandmother seemed to be getting along just fine and I felt like she wanted to be alone so, I asked her if that's what she wanted. She replied, "well, I wouldn't mind being alone for a while, but if you need to stay you can." I didn't need to, in fact, I was ready to have my own again and get back to this thing called life. So, with grandma not needing me there, I moved. I visited her a couple times a week though.

In the meantime, I was back to working, making more money, $25/hr. at that time in 2007, which was pretty damn good. I lived in Downey, so it was an upgrade from Long Beach for sure. Not to mention, I was still dancing on the weekends in Stockton. Once I found the money, that's where you'd find me. I could work any job you gave me, that's a fact but nothing is truer than my hustle, as far as I'm concerned, I was unmatched. So much so, that I had been placed on the billboard and on the business cards for the club.

I mean, shit got out of hand, you hear me? When people started finding out they could see the girl on the billboard actually perform, it was a game changer because everybody knows that the girls that pose for the clubs are porn stars. And let me tell you, the attention was not limited to just men. No, no, no...The women would come in too, wanting lap dances and here's the best part, they would come in with skirts and no panties, begging for me to take them to the back and do anything to make them cum, and they'd come in groups to have me sign my autograph on their breasts with marker and take pics with them. I was quite the sensation for a while.

I had the full support of my family too, believe it or not. Any one of you would've loved my family. Full of laughter, bullshit and non-judgmental good times. My grandma and mom came down to see me one time, mind you, I danced fully nude so when they walked in, I happened to be on the stage butt ass naked. Grandma was wasted, so wasted, she took her shirt off and her bra, climbed on the stage and pranced around the pole, swinging her bra around, yelling, "I taught my granddaughter everything she knows." I swear, that moment was thee highlight of my life. You couldn't tell me shit about my grandma, she was my best friend and could do whatever the hell she wanted.

So, when she asked me to buy one of them vibrating things for her, I didn't hesitate. Say less horny old lady, I got you. I got her a little purple bullet and some batteries. When I got her home, she went straight to the room, I swear she was in there for hours. My mom came by looking for her, I said she's in the room with her new little friend. My mom was pissed that I bought her a dildo. Lol. She was close to 70 but she had a sex drive out of this world.

And she didn't have a problem telling me about it. I loved that grandma was so open with me. We were so much alike, maybe it was the Libra in us, I can't call it, but I loved our relationship and closeness. She told me stories about her and grandpa, I didn't care to hear. Like the time grandpa was looking for the Vaseline in the dark and accidently grabbed the Vicks. My grandma said her sinuses had been clear ever since. But she also told me about the family secrets too. How her daddy used to molest her and that he impregnated her with

Uncle Jhonny and made her give him away. She struggled with that emotionally for years. And even though we found him, she struggled with whether or not she wanted to see him. They never got that chance.

Anyhow, It meant a lot to me that my family supported my hustle because I did enjoy that fast money, I enjoyed it for 14 years. And I was good at it too. I was never bougie, I considered myself a humble opportunist. I knew how to get my money without acting like a bitch, so to speak. I treated my customers like they were my friends and because they didn't feel like they were being used, they'd keep coming back. I'd let them vent and then make them feel good with one of my smooth lap dances. Stroke their ego, act like they were the most attractive men I'd ever seen. And like I really cared about their feelings. It's all a part of the game.

There was something about stepping out on that stage and commanding the attention of the crowd and being able to pull a client from their cash flow from across a crowded room. And if I had some drinks in my system it was even better because I felt more seductive. It was easier to have tunnel vision that way.

A lot of the girls were doing coke at that time. My mama was an addict and so it wasn't something that interested me. But give me a blunt and it's on. I didn't give a fuck who was out there. That stage fed my ego, it allowed my artistry to flow. I loved to dance all my life, so getting paid to do what I loved was a bonus. And looking at naked women all day made me appreciate the beauty of other women. I'd watch my co-workers move gracefully across the stage, some better figures than others, nonetheless, all beautiful in their own way

Chapter 8

We all had a story, we'd sit on the patio, smoke, drink and tell those stories on slow nights. Some girls paying their way through college, some homeless and paying for motels by the night, some on drugs supporting their own habits instead of begging and some just like me, leaving abusive relationships and just trying to get back on our feet. Some of us had kids to feed, some didn't.

I think I'd always had a thing for women, it just became more prominent when I could look at coochie all day. My first experience came from a woman some years prior when I was only 21. We danced together at another club, she was tiny and cute, looked like a younger version of Lil Kim. We got along very well, spoke on a regular basis, but one night we were in the dressing room together and while across from each other, she asked me, "Ice, when you gonna let me eat your pwussy?" I laughed it off as I didn't realize she was being serious.

Next thing I know, she's behind me kissing my back with her arm around the front of me with her hand in my panties, touching me. We ended up on the floor, she had my legs back and tongue inside me. It didn't help that she knew exactly what to do. I was losing it. It felt so good to me. Suddenly one of the girls came back there and saw us, next thing you know, all the girls are in the dressing room around us, watching. Our manager, hearing the commotion, came back there too. He was shook, he saw us and then practically ran out. Probably back to his office to zoom in on the cameras. We finished. Then we all went back to work as usual.

But that first experience didn't make me want to pursue women at all. It was just that, an experience. I think the fact that I always liked women is what prompted me into sleeping with them. Because for 3 years straight, that's what I did, sleep with multiple women. Every weekend that I was out in Stockton, I had a different woman in my hotel room. Mostly girls I worked with. They knew I slept with women and because we were all like family in there, it made them comfortable enough to ask me if I could fuck them and give them their first experience. And I did. I fucked some of my female customers too. Some married, looking for some sideline fun.

My love making style was very slow, sensual and easy. So, it didn't take much of that before the ladies were acting crazy. I was very skilled at what I did. I mastered eating coochie. There was something about a woman squirming, trying to get away because it felt too good, that really just turned me on. I still loved men very much but at that time in my life, I was having fun with women. My encounters with women were just based off sex, nothing more.

After sex was over, aint no spending the night, no cuddling, no holding hands in public. Having sex with women was a thrill for me. And it was something I indulged in privately. I didn't like women in the sense that I respected them. And because I didn't. They were attractive and that was it. I couldn't really be friends with them without taking their panties off. Because in my mind they were all hoes. And maybe that stemmed from my childhood, I saw my mama do tricks. I think it fucked my whole thought process up. My male best friend used to tell me all the time I have the mindset of a man. I used to make these women cry and I'm not proud of that. I've been told I lack emotion and that's so far from the truth. I did care, there were times that I cried over the things I had to do to them, behind closed doors it affected me. My moral was so much better than that.

It fed my ego to know that these women were not only fighting over me but literally becoming sprung. I had one white girl. A couple Hispanic girls, a bunch of black women, red bones. The white girl was crazy, she didn't want to and wouldn't leave my room. We were friends at the club but that was our first night together. I had to go talk to her at her car and make her leave. The Hispanic girls, I didn't like em much. The red bones did it for me. Crazy as fuck though.

I ran into an old classmate up at the club, she came up there to audition at the one in Carson.

Hadn't seen her since high school. Always had been a beautiful girl. I wasn't into girls back then though. We sat on the patio, talked, and did some catching up. The more we drank, she started flirting with me and sitting on my lap. Giggling at just about everything I said. I figured she was drunk. I didn't think she was into women at all. Just having fun.

So, when she asked if she could leave with me after closing, I figured she just wanted to keep drinking and felt comfortable with me because she knew me. So, I agreed but let her know I was going to my male best friend's house to hang and sip with him. My best friend didn't expect me to bring anyone so when I showed up with her, he assumed I brought her for him. He was all excited for nothing. Was upset because she was all in my face. He decided to go to bed and said to me, "Nik, you know where the blankets are." But he wasn't slick, I saw him standing there with the bedroom door cracked, waiting for some shit to pop off.

And did, this girl kissed me and asked me to make love to her. And how could I say no to such a beautiful face. We started kissing and then I went down on her nice and slow, taking my time. I saw my homeboy at his door, jacking off while we did a 69. So after we finished, I took her home. Next day she caught me kissing another girl and caused drama at the club. First of all, the girl I was kissing was the homegirl and she just wanted to know what it was like to kiss a girl, so I showed her, no biggie. I was a whole Casanova back then, of course, I was irresistible. We got into it, she starts yelling at me in front of customers saying..." So this is what you do, fuck me and then someone else? How many of these bitches have you fucked?" I grabbed her by her arm and dragged her to the dressing room. We got into it, I told her to leave, as she was compromising any potential cash flow in that room. Told her ass not to come back and I cut her off. She left the club, I never saw her again.

While working at the club and making lots of fast money had its advantages, there were also disadvantages. I had a friend that worked there for many years. She was hanging out with this customer all night. He wasn't getting any dances or paying her. I think she liked him, but she knew better. Attractive or not, he got to pay up or you moved on to another customer. Well, she didn't, in fact, she left with him that night. I figured she was going to do a private at a hotel. That's what we did on the side. One on one shows.

This girl worked every day, rain or shine, she was always there. So, when she didn't show up the next day, we all thought it was odd. But it was even more odd when a week went by, and no one had seen her. The cops ended up coming in there, I figured some new booty got caught selling ass to a narc and was about to get arrested. No, they were there to question all of us about her. Find out what we saw that last night she was there. I asked if she was ok, they said her body was found in the L.A river, just up the street, a couple days after she left and that there was a murder investigation.

My boss gave surveillance footage and we told them what we knew. We were all scared for a while after that. Some customers were just plain weird. I had a customer I had to fight off in the VIP room, he was choking me and wouldn't let go. Had one that paid me to stomp on his penis with my stilettos while he lay on the ground. I'd do it, he'd leave and come back a week later for more. I left his crotch bloody one time, he didn't want me to stop but I did. It was getting a little too sick for me. I met another guy that wanted me to talk dirty to him while giving him lap dances, while he referenced me as his mother. All I could think of was, this must be how serial killers and rapists are made, disturbed boys that turned into men and never got help with their sick thoughts.

There were times I did what I had to do to make my money, I never sold my ass, that's what them other bitches was for but sometimes those things would consist of me telling guys to meet me at a motel, and thinking they were gonna get some, they'd show up. Soon as they walked in, the door closed and my homeboy would be right there with the heat, soon as he got in the door he'd be robbed. The mf wasn't gone tell, he's too scared. He aint *gonna call the cops, what he gone tell them, he was trying to buy pwussy, hell nah.*

From time to time I did parties... bachelor, bachelorette, birthday, baby shower or divorce parties. I made lots of money. I was dating a guy named "Money" at one time. And while I was down in Stockton over the weekend, he asked me if I could do a bachelor party for his homeboy that was getting married, that he was holding at his house in Long Beach. I told him yeah. He requested I bring another girl for a lesbian show. So, I asked around the club to see who was game for this party. I couldn't get anyone, it was just way too far.

But there was this new girl, she was 18 but she looked maybe 15/16. I told the owner that I thought she was underage, he told me her I.D said 18 and that was that.. She happened to ask me if she could ride back to L.A with me that Sunday.

I agreed but only if she would do this show with me. So, she agreed. We wore red polo shirts and red hats that read "Domino's Pizza" and showed up with 2 real pizza's We went inside and started our lesbian show. I brought toys and everything. After we finished that segment, I had her finish the show while I got dressed and hung out with Money on the back porch.

We were back there hugging, kissing and cup caking as usual, when we heard screams from inside the house. We both ran in. These knuckleheads had this girl upside down, while holding her legs wide open and pouring liquor down her coochie. The bitch's shit was burning. I got into it with them, cursed all they asses out. Knuckle head ass mfs always doing some stupid shit. Money shut the party down. I had the bitch collect my money and we left.

While in the car, she was crying and she said to me, "I wonder what they would do if they knew I was only 15." Right then, I froze. I stopped the car because I had realized that suddenly, I was in a very bad situation, dealing with this fast ass little girl that wanted to be out in the streets acting grown. With a fake I.D that says she's 18. Even though I didn't know, I'm sure it wouldn't make one difference to her family. I made her give me her I.D and told her if anything happens to me, I'm going to have everyone show up at her family's address and there will be problems. I made her get out of my car, I bounced. Leaving her in my rear view. As far as I was concerned, her poor decisions had me in a compromising situation.

The following weekend I headed up to Stockton as usual. But when I got there, something was different. Even though the club was open, it seemed empty and there was something eerie about it. When I walked in, I was grabbed by the manager and yanked out to the back patio. He began to tell me that the police had just raided the club and put their own surveillance in there. Not more than 10min before I showed up. He said the police came in looking for that girl, she was reported missing by her family, she was a 15-year-old runaway and upon them questioning the dancers, they stated that Ice (me) took her to L.A.

I knew how it must've looked, but now there was an assumption that I had taken her down to be pimped on Fig. They were saying that the club was involved in sex trafficking and that I was the madame, luring these girls in. Because I was on the billboard and business cards, I was overseeing the girls and conducting business for the club's operation. And none of this was true. The manager told me that the police were looking for me and that things were bad. He told me to get the hell out of there, get back to L.A, lay low and that he would call me when the smoke cleared.

Shook I slipped out the back with his hoodie on over my head. Got to my vehicle and jumped back on the 99 freeway smashing straight to the grapevine. Thinking, God get me over that Kern County line, that if I was going to jail, I'd rather it be in L.A County.

I thought about my daughter. About her being taken from me, about losing my job at the hospital, my home, my life. That I would have to register as a sex offender and wouldn't be able to get my daughter back. All because of this little lying ass bitch. I would be facing charges for kidnapping, molestation and pimpin & pandering. My life would be over. I thought hard, I cried even harder while I smashed on that gas pedal. As if my problems would magically disappear if I just went a little faster. I made a call to Money, told him what was going on, he told me to come straight over there so we could talk and figure something out.

I had made it out the grapevine and passed the Kern county line with no sign of any police or highway patrol. Until I got just passed Santa Clarita on the I-5, hwy patrol spotted me speeding, I guess. I was already paranoid, I didn't know if I was being pulled over for speeding or that shit that happened in Stockton and I wasn't taking any chances so I stepped on the gas and gave chase. Still on the phone with Money, he knew I was running. He had his car in the garage ready for me. I was scared no lie. Money just kept telling me that he needed me to get there in one piece.

He had a 2-car garage with 2 doors. One facing the front of his house where he'd pull in and one off the alley where he'd pull out. I had gotten off the fwy, with no sign of hwy patrol following. But I could hear the sirens. We were still on the phone, the garage door was already open when I pulled up, I drove in and he quickly shut it behind me. I jumped out of the car and he was right there. We hugged each other tight, as if we'd never see each other again. I jumped in his car, and I pulled out the back, down the alley and gone. As I dipped down the 710 fwy one of our mutual friends called my phone panicked, said we were on the news. He told me play by play what was happening. The police had Money's house surrounded. I was long gone.

I was headed to the main club in Carson, where I had already talked to the owner, he had my back and my paperwork ready to be picked up. When I pulled up, I was scared, didn't know if I could trust anyone. What if the police were there waiting for me? I took my chances, ran in, got my shit and left. See, my main info was located at the club in Carson, not Stockton so the police only knew me as Ice. They didn't know my name or have any address on me, and I was trying to make sure they didn't get it. I was unsure if they even knew the owner had a second club, but I wasn't taking any chances. I was in and out within seconds. Still on the phone with the homie, still telling me what was going on.

They made an entry into the house, looking for me. They found Money, still in the garage. The homie saw them walk him out in cuffs and put him in the back of the car. Money told me that they would take him to jail but he wasn't on parole so he wasn't worried about doing any real time, it wouldn't be much. He protected me. I never knew a love like that before.

The only thing I could do was lay low. About a month later, I got a call from the manager at the club in Stockton. They found the girl in L.A prostituting. She was arrested, brought to Stockton and taken to a juvenile facility. I was never mentioned when she was being questioned. I was cleared. With that, I could return to work, back to the money. Back to my life. And I did. And Money? He did do some time in county, but when it was over, I was right outside to pick him up. I ran and jumped into that man's arms. Within 6 months he'd get into an altercation in Compton and be killed by a rival gang.

Chapter 9

Meanwhile, while grieving, other things in my life would continue happening. At my hospital job, I was scheduled one night to work a double which meant I would be going in at my regular time 3:00 p.m. and getting off at 7:00 a.m. the next morning. So, I situated my pallet in the front of my tv in the living room, with my blankets and pillow neatly arranged and remote next to the pillow. I didn't have a TV in my room, as I thought it would make me lazy, so my TV was in the living room. And at that time, I was sleeping in the living room because I wanted to lay down and watch TV. Kinda defeats the purpose of me not having one in my room. I know. I've always had obsessive compulsive disorder (ocd) so my home stayed clean, so when I left, there wasn't anything out of place. I went to work.

I got off work and made it home around 7:30 a.m. Upon walking up to my door, I noticed a heart in front of my door, a piece of small paper or cardboard in the shape of a heart. It looked familiar but I couldn't place it. I continued to unlock my door and walk into my unit. I noticed a few things were out of place, but I would debunk them with some sort of logical explanation. Like my blankets being balled up and my pillow being on the opposite side of the pallet that I placed it on. I stood there for a minute and concluded that as I was rushing out the door, maybe I kicked everything. The tv was also on and I figured, maybe I stepped on the remote. But it was on a pay per view channel for porn. Once again, it must've been because I stepped on the remote on the way out.

As I proceeded into the kitchen to put my lunch bag away, I suddenly stopped, as I saw something odd that I could not explain away. I had a breakfast nook for me and my daughter to eat at since it was just me and her. I had a dining room table too but that was for decoration only. It was decorated with purple Martha Stewart dishes, purple goblets and fancy napkins wrapped around the silverware and a beautiful bouquet of flowers as a center piece. Oddly there was one of my fancy napkins sitting on the kitchen counter wet and balled up. I froze. How did that get there? And there was a dish in the sink like someone had eaten something.

As I was standing there, an odd feeling came over me. My thoughts immediately shifted to feeling like someone was in my house. I could feel the energy or residual energy around me. I ran into the kitchen and grabbed a knife and started with a walk through of my place. Literally kicking doors open and checking under beds on some 007 type shit. As I was doing this, I realized that for sure someone had been there.

In my daughter's room, her tv was on a pay per view channel just like the living room tv. In my bedroom, my underwear drawer was pulled open, and my panties were hanging out. It smelled like my body sprays had been sprayed in there. My closet was open, I had books on the top shelf that were moved around, I noticed my journal that was hiding in between the books was missing. That journal had contained all my secrets, kind of like a diary.

In my bathroom, the shower had been used, whoever was there, had bathed. There was semen on my carpet, naked pictures of me spread out, that I had professionally taken. I had a basket of lotions, soaps and stuff on the back of the toilet for decoration, the lotions were missing from it. In my living room, there were my small sample lubricants that I had, empty, laying on the table.

I stopped everything I was doing and called the police, making sure not to touch anything. When the police came, they asked me questions and brought in someone to collect fingerprints. It appeared that the person had entered though my kitchen window. There were things missing too. I had some porno DVD's that were missing, my spare car keys, my I.D. and my work schedule paper that was on the refrigerator.

The detective that came and spoke to me told me that it was a crime of passion and that whoever did that had obviously had some type of obsession with me. He said that the person had obviously spent a long time in my apartment as if he knew I wouldn't be there for a while. But I didn't tell anyone I was working a double. The detective determined that whoever was there was very comfortable and was waiting for me to come home and that he felt like the person would be coming back. I was beyond scared at that point.

    I slept with a butcher knife every night because the detective said that most likely he'd come back and I wasn't taking any chances. I called the cable company with the police report information, trying to find out if anything was ordered on my TV that night and come to find out, $80 worth of porn was ordered within an 8 hour time span. Which means that while I did my 16 hour shift at work, someone had made themselves at home in my apartment. Unfortunately, the phone company couldn't tell me if any calls were made, I'd just have to wait until the bill came.

    In the meantime, I had security at my job walking me to and from my car every day, I was constantly looking out my rear-view mirror while driving anywhere because I wasn't sure if I was being followed. I guess you could say, I was a bit paranoid. And things would be that way for a while. They never caught who did it, they said the fingerprints were no good. I slept with protection and started locking the hallway door at night, that *led to both me and my daughter's room. Just to have another layer of protection.*

It wouldn't be long before I'd start hearing bumps in the night, for a completely different reason. I always loved scary movies, so when "white noise" came out, I had to see it. In this movie, they showed you how to talk to spirits on the other side through recordings. I've always been into the supernatural and so it was nothing to go to best buy and grab a small voice recorder and see if it works.

I wanted to talk to my grandfather. So, I set out to do just that. But not before my mom's friend asked me to take her to the cemetery to visit her mother, I thought to myself, perfect, I'll try this thing out at the cemetery first. While she sat at her mother's grave, I'd walk around with the voice recorder, talking into it, asking if anyone was there, if anyone wanted to say anything. I did this for a while and because the experts said that it took practice before you'd hear anyone come through, I figured I wouldn't get any real results just yet.

But when I got home and listened to the recording, I did hear something, in fact, I heard more than one voice. Although I couldn't make out what was being said, it was definitely someone's voice. I was intrigued to say the least. I talked to my grandmother about reaching out to my grandfather and she was down to try so I called my mom over to grandma's house. When she got there, I decided to close the curtains, light some candles and pretty much set the tone.

All 3 of us sat on the couch, I proceeded to talk into the voice recorder and call out to my grandfather. It wouldn't be long before something started happening. My grandmother had a dog named dobie, dobie started barking and growling at the t.v. we couldn't get him to calm down. It was so bad we opened the curtains and blew out the candles and ended our session. Dobie finally calmed down. We decided to take a listen to the recording to see if we got something.

We did but it wasn't grandpa, what we heard would shock us. We heard dobie barking and growling but we also heard another dog with a huskier growl, it sounded almost multi-dimensional, like demonic. We were freaked out. But we knew it was grandpa's dog that passed away (baby). Grandma said she didn't want to mess with that recorder again.

I didn't either after that, it was too much, even for me, but my troubles with that recorder wouldn't end there. Things began happening in my apartment. The first time I noticed something was while I was on the phone with my mama. Out the corner of my eye I watched my kitchen cabinet door swing open slowly. I told my mama what I had just seen, after that, it was happening daily. Eventually all the cabinet doors were swinging open at the same time.

It appeared as though things were only happening when I was alone, never while my daughter was home. Now normally when I'm getting ready for work I listen to my radio in the bathroom and it's usually on a station that plays R&B. Well, oddly while I was lying in the bed sleeping, the music started playing in the bathroom around 4 a.m. at max volume and it was rock music. I was too scared to get up, but I got up and pulled the plug out of the wall. I didn't even want to be there anymore at that point but I didn't have many choices.

I had developed this habit of keeping the doors shut and when I needed to go into that room I'd crack the door and slide my hand up the wall to switch on the lights before I walked into each room. So one night while on the phone with my mom, I had put down the landline phone to use the restroom. After using the restroom, I turned the lights off and shut the doors but as I was backing out of the hallway, and closing the door I felt something, like an energy rush at me. Like something was trying to lunge at me. I didn't see anything but I most definitely felt it. I ran to the front door and grabbed the phone. Told my mom what had happened, she was trying to calm me down but I was freaked out.

I've always believed in God but had a hard time deciding what I believed as far as different religions and so I decided that I believed bits and pieces of each one and so because I knew that Catholics are the ones that perform exorcisms and believe in demonic entities, it was a no brainer that I should go to a catholic church to seek help. I found one in Long Beach, upon talking to a priest about my situation, he advised me to do a house blessing. He gave me 2 bottles of holy water, a house blessing prayer card and also an arch angel Michael prayer card. He told me how to do it and I was on my way.

Once I got home, I opened the windows so that when I did this house blessing, any spirits would have a way to exit. I had also bought some sage to cleanse the house as well, I went through each room slowly saying these prayers, throwing holy water in each corner of every room and waving the sage smoke though out each room as well. It took a while to do but I was sure that when I was finished it would be effective. And it was for a couple months, nothing happened and I was happy because I loved where I lived and didn't want to leave.

As wintertime had arrived, it was getting cold in my apartment, my heater didn't work because the first year I was there it caught fire, due to the previous kids living there shoving their toys in it. It had gone unrepaired. For some reason it seemed as though my room was always the coldest of every room. So cold you could see the cold air when you breathed in there. I was literally sleeping with multiple quilts. One night while my daughter was across the hall in her room sleeping, I heard her screaming for me to help her. I didn't know what was going on but I was scared to get out of my bed. Then when I got up enough courage, I stood on my bed and leaped to the door, then dashed to her room and onto her bed.

Once on her bed I asked her what was wrong and she said to me that she had seen the white wiggly thing again. Whatever it was, it sounded scary. So I asked her where it was at and she replied that I had just run through it. On God I thought I was the only one experiencing things. I had her dad come to get her to stay with him for winter break from school so I could figure it out.

I was alone and whatever this thing was, it was back and much stronger than before. All I could think of is that whatever this thing was, it must've followed me home from the cemetery. I opened up some sort of door by trying to communicate with the dead.

One night I went to sleep as usual with my blinds cracked open just enough to let some light in from outside. When around 4 a.m. I was awoken by something grabbing my foot and feeling it underneath 3 quilts. As I lay there I saw something out the corner of my eyes, crawling on the side of my bed towards me. It was a black shadow figure. I was paralyzed with fear. I couldn't move, scream or do anything. The only thing that went through my mind was to move that foot that it had grabbed. If I could move that foot, it would know I was awake and would leave me alone. I tried so hard to lift that leg and I did eventually. I kept slamming my leg on the bed to scare it off. It was all I could move and it worked. It disappeared.

I jerked my foot towards me and sat up looking around. Unsure whether or not I was dreaming or if that really just happened, I sat there for a while confused. I called my mama and she answered. I panicked. She stayed on the phone with me for a while. My other line rang, it was my baby daddy looking for a booty call. I was uninterested in what he had to offer but I was scared enough to need him. I answered and told him what happened. He came over so I could sleep, he ended up falling asleep also.

I woke up crying badly. I had a dream that my family was taking my daughter from me and putting me into a mental home. It felt so real, it scared me enough to not talk about what was happening to me anymore, for fear that people would think I was crazy. But I wasn't crazy. This was really happening to me. And with what had taken place the night before, I was ready to leave. I was fighting with myself because I knew that if I went to my mom's tiny house, me and my daughter would be sleeping in the living room, because my brothers were also there, along with her ex-husband, his girlfriend and their child. My grandma had found her a 40-year-old boyfriend that was now staying with her. So I didn't want to disrupt her groove.

I started staying up at night and sleeping in the daytime. I had become scared of the dark, I still am to this day. As New Year's started to approach, my aunt wanted to know if I wanted to go out that night. I needed to get away from that house and distract myself somehow, so when New Year's Eve rolled around, I headed out with her for some good ol fun. We went up to Monty Cristo in Hollywood. We had the time of our lives. We stayed until closing and we went our separate ways.

I was jamming to my music on the way home, still pretty tipsy, I admit. As I started to go over the hill on Florence ave. just before old river school rd. it dawned on me that I had to go home and I immediately felt depressed. I pulled into the dark parking lot and proceeded to my door.

I opened my wooden gate and then my front door. When I pushed open the front door something caught my attention right away. I saw a black silhouette crouched down in my kitchen. It was there, the ghost. I knew it was, it was waiting for me to come home. Like it was my man or something. I was so freaked out I ran back to my car, leaving my front door and gate wide open. Anyone could've robbed me blind that night and I wouldn't have cared.

I drove from Downey to Long Beach, to my mama's house. I knocked on my brother's window, he was in there asleep. Him and my cousin. They both got up and let me in. Wondering what was wrong, I told them. They immediately got their shoes on but I didn't want to go back home, ever again. They talked me into at least taking them down there to lock my doors. So I did. When we got there and walked up to the door. They tripped out because I had really left everything open. When they got to the door they saw it too. The man crouched down in the kitchen. He never moved. My cousin had enough balls to walk in and across the room to turn on the lights. I was shocked to say the least, that the silhouette we were seeing was merely my chair turned another direction with my jacket on the back of it. That made me look crazy to both my brother and cousin.

I lived alone, I never put that chair or jacket there, this thing did and now it was trying to make me look crazy. I knew it was time to go. The next morning, New Years day of 2007, I rented a U-Haul and started packing up the truck. I went to my grandmother's house for a while until I figured out where I'll move next. Luckily this thing didn't follow me, I was able to get on with life.

Chapter 10

While at grandma's I got back with this man that I had started dating when I was 13 years old, back when I was in middle school. We were off and on for 14 years, in between other relationships and children, we'd get back together throughout the years only to part ways yet again over differences. Well, this time he had decided that he wanted to marry me seeing as we had been dealing with each other since childhood. And so, when he got on his knee, I said yes. We were physically making our wedding plans, our honeymoon plans, I got my wedding dress, he got his suit, we were ready. When his baby mama decided that because he didn't want to be with her, she'd call the police and tell them that he hit her when he was in fact with me that night. It didn't help that her and his parole officer were besties. I found that out when I got into his voicemail to retrieve the message she had left him, proving his innocence. I took that recording to his parole officer and it disappeared.

I stayed down for him while he was away, went every weekend to chino to visit but he decided that he would make amends with her, I guess so maybe he could get out of jail and when she sent me the letters, it was over between us and I needed to leave my grandmother's house because I knew my ex-fiancé would be getting out and I didn't want him finding me and trying to get back with me. So, I moved again.

It had been a year since I'd left the hospital, the workload was stressing me out, the other nurses I was working with were ridiculous, I just needed a break. So I quit. What I should've done was take a leave. Still dancing at this time, we hit the great recession of 2008. Many of my customers had lost their jobs. Money was very scarce, I tried to go back to work and couldn't, as many were being laid off.

I decided to try a different type of club, a different atmosphere. So I went and got a business license for the city of Anaheim. I ended up at a club that mainly consisted of white folk, where local motorcycle clubs would be at. And where they played rock music and had a very different type of clientele than what I was so used to. So I found myself trying to be as versatile as possible to get the money. I had to become what these other women were naturally. And even though I knew nothing about the latest rock music and hadn't the slightest clue of what I'd be performing to, I did know a little something about classic rock.

I remembered music from my earlier years that I happen to like, like Phil Collins, Michael Bolton, Guns n roses, Aerosmith and Poison to name a few. I figure maybe I could get away with this, swing my hair around and thrash around like the other girls.

And so I did, and I made my money for a little while until one night something happened.

It was a typical Saturday night, I picked my set to go onstage after the next girl. Ordered my Malibu rum as per usual and I knew better than to leave my drink anywhere. I sat at the bar sipping my drink being observant of my surroundings as I usually did and with my glass cupped in my right hand I turned my body to the left to watch one of the girls hit the stage. While watching her I continued to sip my drink.

Reaching almost halfway down the glass when I started to feel something. I felt very strange, as if I was suddenly the most wasted I think I've ever been. But how could that be? I drink the same drink every day, clearly I should know how quickly this drink will hit me, it surely didn't taste any stronger than usual. Right away I started feeling as if I'd been drugged, in fact there was no other way to explain it. I sat there trying to gather my thoughts. My glass was in my hand the entire time, I never let go, but wait, I was turned around watching the girl on stage and there was a man sitting behind me.

Suddenly I started to feel very paranoid, I looked around the room at everyone. I see the man that was behind me, he's now chatting with a group of men across from me and they appear to be looking at me and laughing. Or maybe I'm hallucinating from whatever was in my drink but I was scared, so scared that I stood up and with my stilettos on walked to the bathroom. I locked the door behind me, afraid I would be followed in there. I proceeded to stick my finger down my throat.

I succeeded in making myself vomit and before I knew it, I passed out. I don't know how long I was out, I remember hearing my second song ending, I was supposed to be onstage, so maybe 10-15 min I suppose. I looked to my right and saw my stilettoes on the floor, I picked them up and proceeded to get up, when I fell. I felt even more drunk than I had originally felt. Vomiting was supposed to make me feel less fucked up, it didn't work. I'm scared to open this door, I don't know who to trust. Someone out there wants to hurt me and I'm unclear of whom. I don't know these people, none of them. Their all a bunch of red necks, I see the way they look at me, like I don't belong. I'm much different than them and they don't like it.

Maybe they want to get rid of me, that's what I believed and it terrified me. One might think I should've gone to the manager, or security but what if they're in on it? I made my way out the bathroom and bee lined straight to the dressing room, still holding onto that glass with the contents still in it, I set it on the shelf in front of the mirror. Thinking I'm unable to leave and drive home, I must hide until I can safely get away. I found a huge hole in the wall underneath the countertop, of course it was big enough to climb into but not deep enough to be hidden, I climbed in anyway and passed out yet again. Unable to stay conscious.

When I awoke I was flat on my back being cradled by the manager, he was literally crying and so were some of the dancers. They all stood over me in disbelief. They thought I was dead, just then two uniformed cops walked in asking me questions. Still out of it I pointed to the glass that was still on the countertop. The officer asked, "ma'am, were you drugged?" I nodded my head in agreement. They took the glass with the contents still inside, I was helped to a chair to finish answering questions for the police report.

With the club closing, everyone proceeded to leave. I've now come to the realization that I've been passed out for hours. I was able to get dressed and grab my things despite feeling very much still out of it but obviously much better than earlier. I made my way to the car, security stopped me and said they would take me home seeing as I couldn't drive in the current state I was in.

I decided to take my chances, I didn't want anyone around me, I didn't know what to think. I proceeded out of the parking lot, making it to the 91 fwy. I called a friend to stay on the phone with me. And while I was driving I felt like, considering the situation, it was very probable that someone may be following me. So I drove faster, the lanes on the fwy appeared to be moving in a wiggly type of fashion, luckily it's after 2 a.m. and there weren't very many cars. I made it home and never went back to that club again.

I started up a business where folks could hire strippers for events. I operated from home. Gathered up about 8 girls and 2 armed security guards. Made fliers and business cards. It was booming. But one of the girls was pregnant unbeknownst to me. Her man showed up tryna argue with me that I was tryna pimp his baby mama. So I let her ass go, nobody needs that type of drama. Business got pretty slow after that.

Chapter 11

I ended up going back into security. And then I got lonely again, it had been a couple years so I met someone and entered into yet another long term relationship that went on for the next 9 years, I ended up accepting more than I should have. Doing and being more than I should have ever been to that person. It should've never lasted as long as it did. I have many regrets. What I wanted and what I thought I had was nothing more than a façade. This person was not my type initially but his independence and self-efficiency was alluring to me.

I ended up carrying the entire relationship by myself. That relationship made me miserable, it made me question my self-worth. I cried more tears than I ever thought I had. Over the years I tried having conversations about how I felt, what I needed from that relationship, with no resolve. I argued about things that remained unchanged. The abuse continued. All my secrets and stories of my past being told during pillow talk started being thrown at me in fits of rage. He became close to my enemies and joined in on the gossip about me, while coming home and lying in bed with me like it was okay. He was both condescending and narcissistic.

It was not something I wanted anymore, my love for him kept me there, when eventually hatred started to pull me away. I became who he was to me, I mirrored him so as to give him the same pain he gave me. I no longer wanted to be around him, I'd come home and stick my key in the door and just stand there, not wanting to walk in. I'd turn around and sit in the car instead, for hours. There were lots of arguments because of it. I needed to feel loved and he ignored me like he didn't believe me when I said I had thoughts of cheating. I told him 3 times and things went unchanged. And when we did have sex, I'd imagine someone else so I could climax.

He asked me one time why I close my eyes during sex and I told him, I imagine being with other people. It is what it is, never ask a Libra a question, you'll either get no response or the truth. I was unhappy and unfulfilled. I started asking him if we could start swinging or have threesomes from time to time. I wanted him to be open to that. Really, I guess I just wanted permission to sleep with other people but he wasn't having it.

I kept trying to fix him so I could find my happiness again in that relationship. While trying to fix him, I was only hurting myself. He made no attempt to fix things. It was me doing all the work in the relationship as usual. I knew there was infidelity happening. I knew about him indulging in prostitutes. I worried whether or not it was limited to just women. I had strong suspicions and for good reason. I didn't want him touching me anymore.

And when I stopped caring, we stopped sleeping together, we stopped eating together. We did this for years. Everything he did started to irritate me. We had become so intwined, so used to one another and codependent on one another. He needed a home and I needed his half of that rent and bill money. We tried to make it work. I really tried. He started going through mood swings, affecting everyone in the house. I started feeling depressed and desperate for a way out.

And then one day, I started an argument so I could leave, I ended up at my exes house. Where I'd vent, cry and talk about what was happening at home. Feeling both upset and a bit nervous, I started twisting and pulling at my engagement ring while he held me, rocking me as I cried in his arms. I shouldn't have been there, I started feeling guilty. And then he kissed me, he caressed my body with his fingertips and kissed my neck just the way he knew I liked it, and after a long, intense make out session, he slowly peeled my clothing off one piece after another while he kissed and licked my body.

And then he picked me up and laid me on top of his pool table and just then, my phone started ringing. I was reluctant to answer it, I knew who it was and I was angry, whatever he had to say, I didn't want to hear it. And because I was over it, over it all. It didn't matter what he said anyway. For every single time he stuck his penis in another person that wasn't me, this was payback. Whether he knew what was happening or not.

So when it started happening, I didn't stop it, I didn't hold back. When he stuck his tongue down my throat, I stuck mine down his and as he began to slide inside me, my phone continued to blow up. Text messages flashing across my screen, begging me to answer. "Nichole please, my stomach is turning, don't do this to me." And then my ex took my phone and tossed it onto his couch while shoving himself completely inside of me, sealing the deal.

I let out a gasp, it had been so long, I think maybe 8 months or so. And I laid there while he made love to my body, nice and slow. Giving me exactly what I had been craving for so long. And I cried because it felt so good and I cried because I felt guilty, I felt ashamed. But I continued to love on this man and continued letting him love on me. And when it was over, we fought because I needed to leave. He wanted me to stay with him.

I didn't really know what to expect when I got home. I was aware that I was walking funny, I was low key scared. My feelings all over the place. I gathered up the courage to walk in my door. I saw the holes in the wall, the furniture thrown around. And there he stood, with a look of disbelief he said, "did you cheat on me?" And as I stood there, I must've had this blank look on my face because in almost a trance like state I was remembering all those times I overheard him talking to other women, I remembered the empty condom wrapper that was in his pocket. The messages between him and his exes. All the times he called the police on me and watched me cry while being cuffed for defending myself after he'd hit me. And right then, I made it okay to myself.

I looked up at him still standing there, waiting for my response. I'm not a good liar and I wasn't about to admit anything either so, I said, "What difference does it make? You aint going nowhere anyway." And I proceeded to the bathroom to take my shower. At that point, I think we both knew it was officially over, for the next couple years it would be just like that, moments filled with unanswered questions. I watched him cry and walked right past him just like he did to me. And then one day I decided I wanted to be completely free from whatever this thing was that we were in. And accepted that I'd struggle alone to pay for everything and did. But boy was I happy, I threw a divorce party, even though we were only just engaged.

Unsure whether or not my ex had anything to do with what happened next, one morning I walked outside to get in my car and go the store for cigarettes when I realized my car was on E. But I had just filled it up the night before. So that means somebody ciphered my shit. I was pissed off. I had to walk down the street to a gas station to buy a gas can and put gas in it. Upon walking home, the police pulled me over, and said I fit the description of someone in the neighborhood that had been seen stealing from someone's back yard. What??? That's the dumbest shit I ever heard, but I complied with the questioning. He asked me if I had any drugs on me. I don't sell drugs & I've never done drugs.

This mf didn't believe me, he called a female officer out. But this bitch did more than just give me a pat down, After doing a normal pat down, this bitch opened the front of my sweatpants, pulled my panties open and told the male officer to hold my panties open for her. He did, while she proceeded to stick her hand between my coochie lips, bare handed, no glove.

And then, the bitch put her finger inside me and swiped around, I guess looking for drugs. They did this to me in public, which is unlawful. A cavity search is done at the precinct not in public. I was embarrassed and humiliated. There were no grounds for them to treat me this way. People were driving by looking while I yelled, cursed and cried. They had nothing on me and upon running my name, they saw I had no record of ever being arrested. They let me go.

Hours later I was filing a grievance against the police dept. I should've called a lawyer but I couldn't afford one. I was angry. I wanted those officers fired. The sergeant was the one that took the report. In fact, he came to my house to do it, which was odd as fuck. He said they would investigate the allegations and in the meantime, the officers would be suspended WITH pay.

Great! They gave them a paid vacation. And not long after, I'd receive a letter in the mail saying that the officers were found to be in proper protocol and That there would be no reason to continue the investigation. Angry wasn't the word, They get away with everything but what was I to do? Things were happening on the home front that required my attention at that time as well.

Chapter 12

My brother Michael called me and told me that we needed to take grandma to her doctor for some results from some previous testing that she'd done. We all needed to be there. Grandma was the healthiest person I'd known. She was never sick so it was a bit concerning when she fell ill suddenly. The doctor came in while we patiently waited and when he did, the news would be life changing. She had been diagnosed with pancreatic cancer. The doctor said she had 6 months left to live. She'd only live for 3. She acted as if nothing were wrong. She was as normal as ever, as if she'd accepted her fate. As a family we decided to make more memories with her before she'd leave us for good. We took many pictures.

My family took her to Pechanga to gamble, she loved gambling. I took her to the park where we used to have the union hall picnics with grandpa. We used to dance in front of everyone every year, from when I was a little girl, everyone loved watching us Waltz. Me and grandma loved it the most. It was like we bonded when we carelessly danced together. We carved our names on a bench, talked & watched the squirrels run up and down the tree. And even though it was a little harder for her to move around, she got up and let go of that walker to dance with me one more time. After a few songs she was tired and so she let me video tape her while she told everyone she loved them. It was emotional to say the least.

One morning I got a call that grandma wasn't doing well. Something was wrong. I rushed over to find grandma sitting on the edge of the couch, staring blankly, not even blinking. Like she was in some sort of trance. I pulled the coffee table back, sat on it directly in front of her and grabbed her hands. I said, "grandma, are you ok?" Suddenly she looks at me and says, "mama?" It was getting down to the wire and I wasn't ready for this. I had my brother & cousin pick her up & lay her on the bed that we had in the living room for her. She slipped into a coma almost immediately.

My grandma was like a mother to me. She was like my best friend too. We shared everything with each other. Stories about her life, I knew them all. We were closer than close. I could talk to her about everything. I just couldn't imagine this woman not in my life. The thought killed me. I owed this woman so much. She raised us when my mama couldn't. Gave us a home, holidays, a life. And now, I'll have to live the rest of mine without her.

My mom wasn't in no position to make decisions for my grandmother so I did it. She didn't want to be resuscitated, she wanted to pass away naturally, in her home. And so every day I went over there to spend time with her. Everyone stayed close to her.

Her son moved in at some point to be closer. My mom was there daily. My cousin stayed up throughout the night watching over her. My brother lived there so he watched over her as well. I called in hospice to help out with her and give her meds for pain.

My grandma was already jaundice before she fell into that coma but she became way more yellow, her body began sinking in. She got skinnier. She developed a death rattle before long. Mouth sat open. I'd sing to her. I just didn't know what to do with myself. Even though it may have been silly to everyone else, I felt it may soothe her and so it didn't matter.

And then, that day came. I got the call. Raced over. She was gone. My heart broke. Father's day of 2015. I'll never forget. Me and my aunt cleaned her and got her ready for the mortuary to pick her up. The slamming of the hearse door, closing behind my grandmother is a sound I'll never forget. We all took it hard. Especially my mom. She started drinking way more than she ever had. She collected a total of around $150,000 from grandma's life insurance policy. She could've made a deal with the bank to buy grandma's house with it, seeing as she wanted us to keep the house but that idea went out the window.

She gave a lot of that money away. She used so much of that money, drinking herself to death.

Whoever said, money can't buy you happiness, lied. She found her happiness at the bottom of that bottle. She'd call us (me and my brother's) in the middle of the night, drunk and suicidal. And I never doubted one day she would do something to hurt herself, I mean besides the obvious. She made me emotional sometimes though and so at times, I'd purposely ignore her. At that time I was working a lot of overtime because it kept my mind off my grief with grandma. And well, the company of someone else did too.

My neighbor was always watching me and always making it a point to speak to me. He had lived on the block for a few years. He always had a big smile for me. I'm not gonna lie, I was extremely attracted to him. Not only was he fine but he had a muscular physique. I'm a sucker for a man with muscles. He was always bringing me stuff. No one knew it but we were texting each other low key. He was someone I confided in. We had gotten close at that time. He was there for me when I had no one.

Newly single, I wasn't looking for anything serious with anyone but I guess a girl has needs and he didn't mind meeting them. So, we started sleeping together, regularly. For the next 3 years. I'd go to his apartment or he'd come to mine. We tried to be low key about it. But he was bold, he'd walk right up to me and kiss me if he caught me outside. I aint gone lie, I enjoyed the affection. I hadn't had it in so long. It felt good to be held, kissed, and adored.

He ended up moving at some point. He came and spent the night sometimes. We kept in touch for a while but with us living so far from each other, it really was no point in trying to have some long distance shit. It was time to focus on truly healing myself. Allowing myself to be alone for a while so I could achieve goals, work on my self-esteem.

I needed to fix some things about myself so that I could be a better woman for the next man. And even though I've always been great at communicating, I was never great at following through. And so clearly I needed to work on me. So I did. I read books, meditated, listened to advice videos. As if it were my form of therapy and it really was. I learned a lot about myself. I found a liking in podcasting.

Being able to talk both about my experiences and about my journey in healing, my experience with domestic violence, and being with a narcissistic man allowed me to also help other women. Three years had gone by since my grandmother passed away and I'm barely talking to my mother at this point. She has isolated herself. She is now suffering in silence and I don't think anyone has realized it. I'm working graveyard and pulling overtime to make ends meet. I'm so wrapped up in my life and the duties I have before me, dealing with 3 kids, alone.

I tried to get my mom more involved with her grandkids at some point, by letting her babysit while I worked. She'd get paid for doing it. Putting money in her pockets to pay her bills. But she wouldn't do it if she couldn't drink and so that was that. I had a dream one day, my grandmother came to me. She had never paid me a visit after her passing, although sometimes I'd smell her "Charlie" perfume out of the blue. And while I thought this dream I was having would afford me the opportunity to tell this woman how much I love her. Her visit wasn't for that at all. It was a warning which I did not know right away. In this dream, grandma was standing there staring blankly right at me but as if she couldn't see me. Much like how she had done the day she slipped into her coma.

I was on my knees looking up at her saying, "Grandma? Can you see me? I love you so much grandma." I said it a few times and then she looked down at me. She told me she loved me too. Then she looked forward and started walking away. Only saying, "She's in much greater pain tonight." I knew right away she must be referring to mom. That night I called my mom to tell her about this dream. She sat quietly, then the phone hung up.

I figured I must've upset her. Come to find out, her phone had turned off, she didn't pay the phone bill. It was off for a while. About a month later I got a phone call while working graveyard. It was pops (mom's husband), he said she wasn't doing good. That her feet were swollen and she had trouble walking. That just a week prior he had taken her to the hospital where they said she had severe sepsis, they discharged her with antibiotics to take at home.

Did they not know my mother was an alcoholic and that even if she had taken the meds, she would drink while on them, rendering them unable to work. Her condition was fatal, they were not supposed to discharge her at all. Anyone that has ever been in the medical field knows that. That morning I drove to the east side to go get her and take her to the emergency room. I had her husband carry her to the car. When we arrived, I talked to the staff about what was going on with her. I knew the staff, I used to work with them, they managed to get her a room and admit her. They started her on a round of antibiotics but by that night, she'd be rushed upstairs into the ICU.

The blood infection she had started affecting her organs. Then upon further testing she was said to have end stage liver failure, which in my experience would've only given her a max of 6 months left to live. My mama was dying. Slowly but surely and it didn't matter how much we cried, it wouldn't change a thing. She had abused drugs and alcohol her entire life and when grandma passed away, all she did was drink. No water, no food, just liquor. She lived off that shit. It was eating away at her insides. And with further testing, they found meth in her system. Which gave me and my brother Michael the idea that she knew she was dying. Suddenly it made sense why she looked at me the way she did that day in the emergency room. Like she was silently speaking to me. Her big brown beautiful eyes telling a story of pain and sorrow.

Chapter 13

For the next 2 ½ months, I'd spend my days up there with her. As soon as I'd get off work. I'd go straight there to be with mom, sign whatever I needed to, approve procedures to keep her alive. And spend whatever time I could with her but I knew in my heart she wouldn't make it. I knew in the er that first day. I had my mom sign papers that day to give me guardianship of her, to make health care decisions in the event that she couldn't and because I knew how serious it was. Trying to explain things to my brother's and make them understand what was happening to her was impossible, yet heart wrenching at the same time. How could I tell them that mom was dying and that what we were about to do was watch it all happen. And because we would. We'd see her through till the very end and be at her side like she would've wanted.

While mom lay helplessly in ICU, my nana sat down there in rehab anxiously waiting to go home. So strong and optimistic. She was much smaller than I had remembered. She was doing well though, even though her health wasn't. But just as my grandma had, she kept a smile on her face too. My brother landed himself in the hospital too, 3rd floor cardiac ICU. He was upset about mom and decided to take a walk in the rain. Developed pneumonia and had fluid in his lungs. He fought with staff, wouldn't let them help him. Me and Michael had to go up there and talk to him. Without a chest tube Wayne would die. They put the tube in and drained the fluid.

Every day I visited all three of my family members in the same hospital. And signed paperwork daily for my mom and brother. But two of them wouldn't make it out. My brother Wayne was discharged. Saved only by the grace of God. Nana went in for a procedure on her heart, she didn't make it. I took my kids in to see her the day before. I'm glad I did. Our hearts were broken and I was in utter disbelief. I knew the family couldn't handle two deaths so close. Mom had no choice but to stay alive, at least for a little while longer. We stayed by her side. The loyal children we were. Her husband never left her side either. With moms confusion and slurred speech I had her pray with me and repeat every word very slowly. I asked God to forgive her of her sins so that she may dwell in the kingdom forever. But I knew it would need to come from her. I can say proudly that mom managed to utter those words.

She started seeing grandma at the end of her bed. I can only assume she was waiting for her. She said, "grandma is mad at me, she won't talk to me, she just stands there." I said, "Mom, I don't think she can talk now but she's here to watch over you ok." I couldn't see grandma, but I'm sure she was there. I looked over at the end of the bed before leaving that day and with teary eyes, I told her, "thank you grandma."

Mom deteriorated slowly, but on some days she seemed better, I knew what was happening. It was "the surge before death", also known as "terminal lucidity." Which happens in people that die a slow death, as their body has opportunity to shut down on its own. And that's what was happening to her while we waited for a miracle.

Her body had enough. Her severe sepsis turned into septic shock. Her only kidney was barely working, they stopped her dialysis. Her heart was being affected, her brain, her legs swelled up like balloons. Her toenails started falling off and blood vessels started bursting underneath her skin, her arm was black because of the blood underneath. Mom's eyes were fixed open, she stopped blinking and went into a comatose state. Her body and eyes were orange as her liver had started dying.

I couldn't watch her in pain anymore. I think we all silently knew it was over. When I looked in my mama's eyes, she wasn't there anymore. As if we were just praying over a shell, her spirit had already gone on. Or maybe it was lingering just above us, waiting for us to let go. And on one Wednesday afternoon, we did. We didn't have much of a choice.

I asked the doctor to put her in a deep sleep, which she most likely already was. I asked him to give her a cocktail of drugs so she'd go out high as a kite. And after a while when everything would've had time to kick in, I had them silence her machine to not make any noise and take her off life support. Michael and Wayne walked out, they couldn't take it. Me and my baby brother stayed to see her all the way through. We cried and waited for her to go on her own, I guess you could say. And she did, 2 ½ hours later. I'd like to think she must've been bargaining with God during that time, maybe she watched her life memories flash before her as she lay there.

Pops turned to me and just cried, I hugged him and while hugging him, I felt an ache in my heart that I still, to this day cannot describe. I felt my mom die, as if a spiritual umbilical cord had been severed from between us. I felt it. Even before I looked up at the monitor. I heard myself scream and as I peered over his shoulder, I saw the flat line. She was gone and I passed out. My cousin told me she grabbed me and when I came to, I was face down looking at the hospital floor, reaching for a trash can to vomit in.

That was the second time I had realized that death does something to my nerves and makes my stomach turn. The first time was nana. We stayed there for a little while after she passed, talking to each other. We kissed mama goodbye one last time and left. Michael waited for me in the parking lot. We hugged and cried. The way that boy cried, it hurt my soul. My job as a big sister was to always protect him as well as my other brother's but I couldn't protect them from that pain. We would go through that pain together.

I had a funeral to plan, video's to make, decorations to pick out. Obituaries to make. We gathered up the money we could, family sent money from near and far to cover that service which came out pretty amazing. My baby brother gave up his taxes for it. Michael bought the urn and a bunch of keepsake necklaces. We did a service with her cremated. I didn't want my mama being seen in a casket the way she was, she had deteriorated so much within that 2 ½ months, she went from 55 to 86 real quick and I couldn't let her be seen like that. She would've haunted me for the rest of my days for that.

We all grieved in our own separate ways. We all took it hard, we all felt guilty for not being as much as we could have been for her in her last months leading to her death. We surely didn't think we would lose her anytime soon. My mama could throw down a handful of pills, (literally at least 8) Vicodin or Norco's at once with a bottle of Jose Cuervo and walk around okay. It boggled us that she was alive after all she was doing to herself. And it didn't matter how many times we tried to talk her into stopping. She just didn't care about her own life enough.

It became hard for us to watch, and so we just didn't. We all had regrets after her death. I want to say Michael took it the hardest, although he used different drugs here and there in the past, it was never enough for me to call him an addict. Not like Wayne, we knew he was an addict. He was open about his drug use. He was a functioning addict. But Michael? No, not Michael, he wasn't like that at all. At least up until mom landed herself in the hospital.

He dived right on into drug use, full blown and it just got worse, he was going downhill fast. Mom's death broke him. He bided his time trying not to think about her, by buying auctioned storage units and reselling the items. He threw it all into my garage and got a kick out of showing me all the cool stuff he came up on. He enjoyed it and so I did too. His addiction got worse and his personality changed. He was going through things, not just with mom's death. He admitted to me that part of the reason he was doing drugs was partially due to his relationship with his girl.

He couldn't deal with her. I saw some of their issues from both sides of the spectrum. My brother was insecure about her and it was because of a rumor that two family members admitted to smashing her while he was in jail on a gun charge.

That ruined the relationship between him and those family members for a while. He stayed with her and had my nephew. He took care of her, her son and their son. My brother was the provider. And his stress levels were through the roof so when mom was dying, he'd show up at the hospital telling me his troubles. She'd be blowing him up as soon as he got there to be at mom's side. Yelling about things.

I had gotten into physical fights with her in the past over the way she treated my brother and even got into it with him on occasion about the way he treated her. They were toxic together. With no support from her, he stayed close to his siblings. As his drug use, grieving the loss of mom and woes at home continued, my brother would go deeper into this dark hole he was in. Even jeopardizing our relationship at some point. He got upset with me needing my garage back and took full vengeance because of it. Enlisted the neighbor that lived in the back that he used to hang out with, to text me and develop some sort of I don't know what. I kept getting text messages from him. I figured it was someone in the neighborhood that had some sort of crush.

My brother knew about the relationship I had previously had with the other neighbor and so he used this guy to make me think he was him. I knew better because I was still in touch with the old neighbor that had since moved out. So one day I called this guy's bluff and while he was texting me telling me to leave my door unlocked and wait for him in my shower, instead of pressing him about who he was like I usually would, I agreed, just to see who he was. I went into the house, kept the screen locked and waited at the door with the wooden door cracked so I could see out.

And low and behold, this big mf comes strolling around the corner and up to my door. He grabbed my doorknob and turned it, only to find it was locked. He stood there confused for a second or two before I unlocked the screen and thrusted it outward, hitting him the forehead. Not realizing at first it was the neighbor in the back that lived next to the laundry room, of whom had a girlfriend that I had associated with on occasion. I yelled, "who the fuck are you?" while walking behind him briskly as he tried to get away.

He stopped on the side of the apartments so as to not let his woman hear all the commotion. He said, "I'm sorry, your brother put me up to it. Up to what though? What the fuck was supposed to happen when got he got in my house? I never got the answer to that. He begged me not to tell his woman and because I knew that living with her must've been his livelihood, ain't no telling what he would do to me if she kicked him out. So I made a deal with him that if he saw my brother, he would make sure to keep my brother away from where I lived or I would show his girl the text messages.

Even trade as far as I was concerned. I didn't see my brother for a while after that. He was okay, he just didn't come by my place anymore. I'd hear about him going back and forth to jail, getting gun charge after gun charge. Doing time, getting out and doing the same thing only weeks to months later. He was putting up posts on face book saying that I murdered his mama and that my face would be the next on a t-shirt.

That wasn't my brother talking though, it was the drugs. My brother loved me, he was my protector, so hearing stuff like that from mutual friends didn't anger me, it scared me. For a long time I thought he would try to kill me. My brother Wayne was going through things with him at that time too. He confessed to me that he was scared of him also. I said silent prayers for my brother as often as I thought to do so. I became suicidal and no one knew about it. I kept it to myself as I didn't want to concern anyone.

Chapter 14

Being alone allowed me to reflect on my mother's death and how it affected me. I often asked myself if I did all I could for her. Many nights I sat there saying to myself that I wanted to die just like her, that I deserved to feel every inch of pain that she felt. And all because I wasn't able to save her. I made her death my fault. But I wanted to change, I wanted help. My world was very silent at that time. There was no help available to me. Michael ended up in jail, he was sober, reaching out to me and I'm sure he didn't remember why we had beef. I wasn't going to remind him, it wasn't important.

What was important was our relationship and for me, working on that was a start. I was sending him pictures and books to read. I was accepting his phone calls. He's my brother and our relationship was important, we both knew that. The apartment I was living in had issues, I had been living there for 10 years. Homeless people were moving into the neighborhood at an alarming rate. Tents everywhere, under the freeway underpass which was right across from my apartment and wasn't very appealing. Someone started setting their tents on fire because they didn't want them in the neighborhood. I was surrounded by different gangs. mostly consisted of people I went to school with.

Things were quiet for the most part until a Mexican gang from Compton started showing their faces, driving through the streets slowly and casing the neighborhood. One of their homies had got smoked just one block over and clearly they were seeking vengeance. Things were getting bad. I was hearing gunshots more frequently. Suddenly there were termites in my building. The owners didn't want to tent the apartments because they didn't want to pay for the tenants to stay in a hotel while it was being fumigated So they did the bare minimum which wasn't enough.

And suddenly out of nowhere, mice began infesting the apartments. The pest control would come out and give me sticky traps to catch these mice and I caught 8 mice on my own. I wanted to move and because of the coronavirus pandemic, I was unable to. I spent most of my time outside, I didn't want to be in the house. I felt like there was a whole plaque going on in there. I was so anxious to move that I started packing, even though I couldn't move yet. There were boxes stacked up in the living room for months.

With nothing happening and no sign of light, I continued drinking all day and all night. More than I ever had. I'd sit in the car and even though, I still managed to do online classes to gain my credentials to elevate my career for when I did go back to work. I did these classes from my phone, passed tests and gained all the certs I needed, while holding a bottle in my hand and being wasted. And after I did that, I started fixing my credit on my own, from my phone and with a bottle in my hand. Brought my credit score from 510 to 765 in 5 months.

I had always wanted cosmetic surgery on my stomach and butt. After years of working out, I couldn't get rid of my c-section pouch and my ass? Well, let's be honest, it started looking like my mama's did which wasn't very flattering. I hated my body and I was very insecure about it. I cried when I looked in the mirror. And I had recently found out that if I had a good credit score, I could get my body work financed and so that's what motivated me to fix my credit. I had all these ideas and goals in my mind that I wanted to do and at that time I was only able to do the small things because all the big things were out of reach.

I needed to move away and start fresh. I needed to stop drinking and smoking. I never had an issue putting the bottle down, I only drank when I was bored. But smoking was a different ball game for me. I started that at 14 years old. I knew that it wouldn't be easy after 26 years of that habit but I really hated smoking at that point, I was over it. And oddly within a week apart, two different men ran up to my car in the middle of the night. Both men I had spoken to at some point seeing as they knew my brother Wayne. Both homeless and on drugs also. They both were running from someone apparently trying to kill them. The first guy said someone was shooting at him and wanted my help. I told him I couldn't help him. The second one a week later said he didn't know some girl had a boyfriend and now the guy is trying to kill him and I said, why you run up to my car? What am I supposed to do? You making me a target, go away.

I didn't know what was going on, are these warnings for something bigger to come? I admit it sounds a bit crazy and as I'm typing this I'm still trippin off it all. It scared me and I started to feel like all of it was happening for a reason. I couldn't shake the feeling that something bad was about to happen to me. I became a little paranoid. I stayed inside my house for a few days just thinking that with all the things I needed to do and wanted to do, I would need a higher power to help me.

I eliminated my distractions and on one day I decided not to pick up a bottle, as I usually would. But instead, I decided that I would spend my day talking to God, praying and pouring my heart out to him. Give him total control of my life and let him lead me to salvation. And what I did was pray and cried harder than I ever had in my life. I dropped to my knees and stayed there for hours. And when I had not a tear left, when I had begged and pleaded all I could, I had given up my free will. But I felt relieved. I went to bed in the middle of the daytime and slept until the next day.

The next morning, my life started to change. I received a phone call that I could put in my notice to move, and I did, immediately. I started gathering documents and everything I needed to move the process along. Stayed on that phone constantly. I got more boxes and continued packing. I decided not to sit in my car anymore at all. Which made me stop drinking too. I slowed down on my smoking, from 10 a day to 1 a day.

I spent many days ordering new things for my new place. I did consultation's for my body work and weighed options. New year's came along, I spent it partying with my neighbors one last time, they helped me chase and corner a mouse that was trying to get some New year's eve action Lol. I didn't make any resolutions but I did promise myself that I would give my problems to God more, instead of thinking I could do everything alone. I opted to live life more optimistically than I ever had before. I decided that my happiness mattered and that from that point on, I would do what made me and these kids happy instead of worrying about making others happy while they couldn't give the same in return.

Finally, it's time to get out of here. Well, that's what went through my mind when me and my homeboy pulled up with the U-Haul. I found out that morning who my friends really were, when a couple of people flaked on me. I guess some folks just don't like money. I had to find other people at the last minute to help me. My daughter had come the night before to grab her brother's so I could get moved without them being in the way. A couple of hours was all it took for me and my two friends to get it done.

From Long Beach to Irvine and back to Long Beach to drop them off. I bought them lunch and gave them $100 each. I was unpacked and settled by the end of the day, thanks to my daughter and her homegirl. Me and my boys slept well that night, in our new home. The feeling was amazing. The sense of relief and accomplishment was everything to me. I had an app on my phone called "citizen". It gives you alerts about what's happening around you and in your neighborhood and I guess I forgot to disable it. It was still set to my old address in Long Beach.

So one week after I moved, I'd receive an alert about a shooting that oddly was on my block, so as I read up on the details of this shooting and proceeded to watch this video, I realized something. Not only did I see a vehicle completely sprayed, it was silver in color like mine. That tripped me out but what really spooked me was that the car was parked exactly in the spot that I parked mine every single night. The shooting happened in the middle of the night. That could've absolutely been me. And was it supposed to be, I mean, was it intended for me? The thought frightened me, that my limp body could've been found behind a bullet riddled car door. If God hadn't got me out of there just one week prior.

Only God could've known what was to come. He saved me and I didn't want to disappoint him in the least for doing so. So, because God thought my life was important, so should I. I wanted to live, I wanted to live long for my children. I wanted enough time to give them a future. It took me another month before I officially quit smoking. But I did it. I started eating right and exercising. I found my surgeon and set the date for early May. Only 2 months away.

I got the financing I needed. 18k to be exact for three procedures that would all be done at once. I remained humble and very aware of the consequences of such an extreme move. In fact just a few weeks before my surgery, there was a woman from Long Beach with 2 small children, like me, that took a trip to Tijuana for the same procedure. She never made it home. She died on the table. I was terrified but I knew God had me and with all the research I had done, I trusted my doctor. He had put me on 2 series of antibiotics 2 weeks before surgery to prevent infection.

The day had finally come. My daughter and son in law took care of the kids for me while I went under the knife for 8 hours. They took me to a room with a gurney full of padding and several staff members waiting with gowns and hair nets on. They took my gown off and washed my entire body with antibacterial soap and laid my wet body down on the gurney. I was so cold. They placed a mask over my face and had me count backwards until I fell asleep.

Chapter 15

I prayed before I knocked out. I don't remember waking up. I don't remember waking up in recovery at all. I don't remember the drive home. I remember seeing my daughter's face. I remember her helping me out of the car into the house. I remember vomiting and I remember the excruciating pain.

The best part for me was seeing my stomach flat. I cried. No more lifting my stomach to shave, no more pulling my underwear and pants over my stomach and wearing baggy shirts to hide it. And my ass? I wasn't sure what to think of it. It was shaped different and definitely bigger. It was exciting to say the least. My dimples were still there though but I got over it. I was happy looking at myself and that's what mattered. While the kids finished up their school year online, I enrolled the kids in school for the New year in Irvine.

2021 was a new year full of change for us. It was a year filled with optimism and lots of smiles. But then more things started happening. With the good came the bad. The highs and the lows. The devil was busy trying to knock me down again. It was time for me to go back to work, a person that I thought was a good friend, had promised me a good paying job, that after getting all my certs and gun license for, I would be able to have. The certs I had obtained were specifically for that job. This job had the right pay, right hours, etc...But all that came to an end abruptly when it was time for me to actually get that job. Which I desperately needed being that I was a single mother and my living expenses would cost a bit more seeing as I moved out of the hood. Let's be honest, it's expensive as fuck living in Irvine.

As I notified him that I would be filling out the app, I noticed that he didn't have a direct link for me to apply. I googled the company and found that there were no positions available and that particular post wasn't listed either. The starting pay was much lower as well. Did he lie to me as a way to be more involved in my life for that whole last year? I wondered because the way he acted about it was odd. It was as if he showed no concern for his misinforming me.

He had plenty of time to tell me that they weren't hiring or even enough time to tell me he was full of shit, but he did neither. Instead, his reaction when I told him that there were no positions listed for his post was, "Well what do you want me to say?" Then he went on to tell me about his day at work, at the same place I should be starting work at. I didn't want to hear that shit. As far as I was concerned, he didn't have the pull or power he claimed to have had.

He was unable to pull any strings or do anything. And because he lied to me and showed no compassion for how he mislead me and upset me, our friendship was over. Who needs friends like that? I needed to find a job elsewhere and fast. My Edd was ending quickly and my bills and rent needed to be paid. I finally landed a new job which was more pay than my last job but not as much as I felt I should've been making. It would work though. I enjoyed it, I worked alone and the hours worked for me.

My brother was released from jail. For the first time in a while, me and my brother were able to talk and even spend a little time together catching up. He admitted to me that he used some drugs when he got out, some that he stashed before he left. I didn't judge him. I wanted him to feel comfortable enough to talk to me and he did. He was going through so much at home with his baby mama and he was still so very upset over mom's death even though 2 years had passed.

My brother was fighting his addiction and he was fighting hard. He was getting into it with his baby mama so much and calling whomever he could in the middle of the night to get himself away from her. I felt like things between them were coming to an end. My brother wanted his life back. He told me, my brother and our cousins all about how he was going to do it. And we were there for it. He came to my house and stayed with me for 3 days. I cooked for him, he ate so good over here. He wasn't eating at home. He started telling me everything he was going through. He was being put out every other day and there was a concern that his bm was sleeping with her brother that she had living there with them.

The first night was the hardest though. He cried so bad that first night. He kept saying he wanted mom and he kept saying F*** God for taking her. He repeated it over and over again. It scared me because you don't disrespect God like that. I felt like God would punish him for that. I immediately started praying over him. He dropped to the ground in position to pray and I laid over his back and held him while I prayed. Out of nowhere he rose up and threw me off of him. It was at that moment that I felt like my brother was fighting something. I honestly felt like he had a demon on him.

His baby mama continued to blow my phone up, trying to fight with him. He wasn't saying a word to her and she just kept at it. I was able to see everything firsthand that he had been telling me for years. She had even started being disrespectful towards me for picking him up, as if I should've let him sleep on the streets after she kicked him out. Even though I was cool with her, I didn't owe her my loyalty. My brother was always going to come before her. After the 3rd day, I took my brother back. I should've kept him with me and I wish I had.

In the meantime, my car that was 2 car notes away from being paid off started having issues. It started over heating and fast. I couldn't drive it to the next light without it smoking. One of the hoses broke. I took it in and they said one of the head gaskets blew. There was just a whole array of issues with it all of a sudden. I didn't have money to fix it but I needed the car to continue working.

It took a while to get fixed, in the meantime I was getting rides to and from work, paying gas daily. It was a real stressful moment for me. I couldn't get the kids to school, it was too far. The school behind where we lived managed to get them in over there which helped me tremendously because I could walk them to school. And while all of that was going on something else happened that would change my life forever.

I got a phone call about my brother Michael. His baby mama was on the other end of the phone screaming and crying. I wasn't talking to her at that time because of how she acted about me picking up my brother the last time and it had only been 2 weeks. She told me that the ambulance was there working on him and that she thought he was dead. And was he? I didn't know what to believe, coming from her.

She had told me several stories about him falling out, dying and needing cpr to be revived and back to doing drugs later that day. Which sounded odd as fuck to me. This is the first time she has called me frantic, but he dies all the time according to her. The first time was when he got locked up this last time and he had just finished that bid. He had only been out for a couple of months. So for the last few years that he had been doing drugs, he never died from it. Now suddenly he dies every other day and has been for the last couple months. This is what she wanted me to believe.

My other line rang, I clicked over. My baby brother on the other end, panicked. I'm trying to calm him down, he's telling me the same thing. Now I'm running out the door, luckily I had a rental car to do it. I grabbed my youngest from school as he was getting out just then. We headed to the apartments, as the fire dept was on scene working on him still. I'm 30 min away. My mind is racing, I don't know what to think. Will I make it on time, will he even be there? Why are these cars moving so slow on this freeway?

And then I got another call while I was driving, his baby mama again. They got a faint pulse on him and he's being rushed to West Anaheim Medical Center. I typed in the info on my phone and I headed over. I pulled in and jumped out the car with my son under my arm, I ran into the ER and was stopped by an emt telling me to calm down and asked me who I was looking for. I told him my brother and I needed to make sure he was alive. The staff tended to me pretty fast and took me back to see him.

And there he was, my funny, handsome, charismatic, little/big brother. Laying there, helpless and on life support. Being kept alive by a machine. He was clearly comatose. I spoke to him, I let him know I was there. I requested to see the doctor. I needed to know exactly what was happening and what the plan of care was. She explained to me that they were waiting on a bed to send him to ICU, but there was more.

They lost his pulse twice on the way to the hospital. She suspected major brain damage. He was without oxygen for far too long which can cause brain death. I knew what that meant. She didn't expect him to live past 24 hours. I burst into tears and immediately got on the phone and started calling family and friends to get up there fast.

Chapter 16

In the meantime I had people talking to him on the speaker phone so he could hear them. I needed any bit of encouragement I could get from anyone to make this boy fight. I held his hand while I waited for everyone to come. I talked to him and told him I needed him, I loved him and that he had to fight, he needed to wake up. I stood there in a daze, confused and didn't understand how we got to this place in time that we were in.

He had just been to my house 2 weeks prior, I had spoken to him not even a week ago. He was waiting for his I.D to come in the mail so he could go back to work at the refinery. Our aunt was going to get him in. He was motivated and ready to get his life back and I believed him, in fact we all did. See, one thing about my brother, when he said he was going to do something, he absolutely did it. Why are we here? Sadly I'd never get the chance to have the conversation that would give me the real answers I needed.

My family showed up. I called my friend to grab my other son from school and to bring him to me. I then had my baby daddy come to the hospital to get the boys. My brother was being transferred to ICU. We all flooded the parking lot. And because we didn't know whether or not he would survive the next 24 hours, we stayed all night.

I was the only one that was able to see him at that time because I had my coronavirus vaccine. So I was in and out, giving everyone updates. I recorded voice clips of family telling him they love him and to fight and then I took the recordings up there for him to hear them. We bought lots of liquor and stayed up. We talked, cried and got drunk out there. A few people said they spotted him that day outside the hospital, even though he was in that hospital bed. Maybe his spirit was traveling while his body lay there helpless. Maybe he wondered what we were all doing out there. Everyone piled in their cars to sleep that night, my brother's baby mama slept in my car.

And while everyone slept, I lay in my driver seat staring at the roof of the car. I couldn't sleep. The depths of my soul was deeply disturbed. I got out of the car, paced the parking lot for hours, called up to see how my brother was, several times. I cried, I vomited, I prayed and repeated that cycle throughout the night. I thought to myself, how could this be happening? We just lost mom only two years ago. We can't lose Michael too. He survived that 24 hours and another 3 days after that. We all went back and forth the entire time.

Dad and sis flew out, one from Florida, one from Jersey. As my brother just got worse and worse. We were waiting for the brain scan to come back, to see if there was any brain activity. We were told that because he had gone without oxygen for so long, that his brain was so injured, if he wasn't already brain dead, he would be a vegetable. Either way, things weren't looking good for my brother. He had really fucked up this time, I had thought to myself. Initially, me and my youngest brother had a conversation about putting him in a convalescent home near us, and that we would be there every day to rehabilitate him, if his brain wasn't too damaged and he could possibly recover. We were willing to put in the work.

But then we found out that it was much worse and that he wouldn't recover, he would be totally paralyzed, unable to speak or do anything, due to the damage. We still waited for the brain scan. While we waited, our brother developed an infection throughout his body. His brain started leaking fluid, down the back of his neck, damaging his brain stem. He was burning up. If he wasn't already brain dead, his brain would fry from being overly hot.

They stripped his gown off and covered him in ice blankets. My brother never woke up. He twitched and made faces while his brain started to die. We had hope because as long as his lungs were at least partially working, he had some brain activity. But on my birthday, his lungs stopped. Me and my baby brother talked about taking him off life support. But we'd wait a day or two.

I spent my birthday with my brother, I laid on his lap and cried my eyes out. I begged him to wake up, I held his hand and told him how much he meant to me. I continued to speak to him. I knew if he couldn't do anything else, he could hear. I talked about special memories we had together, even the funny ones. I went back and forth outside to drink the Hennessy my baby brother bought me. My family low key tried to give me a birthday at the hospital, flowers and cards. And all I wanted was to give them to my brother, but they said they weren't allowed up there.

Family members started slowly coming up to see him. Some already had vaccines, others were running out getting one and others, well, they did what they had to do to get up there. I allowed ex-girlfriends to come up there, old classmates from elementary, middle and high school showed up. He had such an abundance of love around him. But even that wouldn't be enough to save him.

The following day, he was pronounced brain dead. I like to think he went on his own, so we wouldn't endure the pain of taking him off life support. In the end, he got what he wanted. To be with mom again. My brother signed up to be an organ donor, and as a result, he saved 3 lives. I learned that one of them was a baby. Which afforded him the privilege of getting into those golden gates.

At least, that's what I like to believe, as a God fearing woman. If he had to leave us, I wanted him to be with God and the rest of our family. That was important to me. That he made it. We had a hard time with that loss, we fought, argued and cried. And as Michael had gone on to transition from one life to another, he made sure to mess with me one last time that same night. By slapping my blinds in front of everyone, making them swing back and forth. We all saw it. We didn't get scared, we didn't run. We looked at each other and simply said, "and there goes Michael."

I had a funeral to plan, so while I waited for his body to be released, I started planning. He loved the 49ers and so I wanted to honor that. I wanted it to be a service to remember. I managed to get up the money, it was amazing. But that day, after all the hard work and holding back the tears so I could finish, I had officially broken down. I went in to view his body to make sure he was perfect, before the service. Seeing my brother in that casket made his death a reality. It hurt like hell to see him like that and I couldn't hold the hurt in. My brothers were distraught also.

There were rumors going on about my brother's death that needed my attention. A friend of my brother came to tell me that the rumor that was going around was that my brother had gotten into an argument with some other people in the apartment complex, a few weeks before his death. No one knew what that argument was about.

When he was found that day, he was on a back stairwell that led to a carport in the back of the apartment. He was slumped over, blue in the face and not breathing. But what was said is that he was walking to the liquor store to get my nephew some juice, when those guys he got into it with pulled up on him. For whatever reason, he got into the car with them.

I know my brother, the only reason he would have gotten into that car was if he felt like his family would be in jeopardy if he didn't. They drove him to the store to get the juice. My brother came out of the store and got back into the car. He was driven back to the apartment but before he could get out, they stuck him with a needle and propped him up on the stair well with a makeshift foil pipe next to him, to make it look like an overdose.

I didn't know what to believe. I was angry. Me, my dad, my baby brother, some family members and a few other people felt like something wasn't right about his death. That feeling never went away for me. As I'm writing this, I still feel it very strongly. I went to the police with what info I had. I had an address on these people, after research, I had names of the people that lived there. The police did nothing, they said it was here say, they wouldn't even investigate it.

Because my brother had been arrested with narcotics before, he was known to them as a drug addict and a repeat offender. I guess that made him less worthy of proper treatment. That was the beginning of my crusade to get justice for my brother and find out the truth. I requested police reports and 911 call logs. I heard the actual phone call that came in for my brother. It was heart wrenching to hear the manager of the apartments say that she didn't want to touch him to do cpr after the dispatcher directed her to. She could have saved his life and chose not to.

I requested the coroners reports and medical records from the hospital. My brother did not die from an illicit drug overdose, as the coroner suggested on his death certificate. There were no illicit drugs in his system. Upon talking to the coroner herself, she said that she put that on the death certificate because the police had said to her that they believed it was a drug overdose he died from.

Chapter 17

I waited for the medical records from the hospital to tell me something, anything. And as far as what I read, I didn't see that there were any tests done to determine whether or not he had drugs in his system. It's a mystery I wasn't willing to give up on. Five months had passed since his death and while we weren't over it, it was starting to get easier. I went from crying multiple times every day, to maybe a few times a week. I kept searching for answers. I drank quite a bit and every time I did, I wanted to sit outside those apartments and watch that apartment and wait for someone to come out so I could stick them with a needle and kill them like they did my brother.

After receiving Michael's death certificate I went to go retrieve his 3 storage units that contained all of our family memorabilia. Grandmas photo albums from her childhood, our childhood, along with other family members photos. The rest of grandmas remains were also in there. Some items from her home. My mother's belongings from her home as well. Of course my brother had a lot of his stuff in there also. It was important that I get into those storages because I had 3 family members belongings in there that are no longer alive. Our family memories are locked inside those units.

When I got there the people in the main office notified me that his storages were auctioned off months prior to my brother's death, even before he got released from jail, due to lack of payment. Well that's crazy and that can't be right because my brother left his baby mama $6,000 to cover those storages while he was away. So when I confronted her about not paying for the storages, all she had to say was that she needed the money for bills. Okay, understood, but she received mail regarding those storages, she knew they were being auctioned. Not once did she ask me to help pay for them. She didn't offer for me to take over payments or go retrieve the important things that belonged to my family. She said nothing, she didn't care, it wasn't her family's stuff. Just like that, our memories were gone due to her lack of consideration for the family that took her and her son in.

Trying to keep from being angry enough to ring her neck was one of the hardest things I had to do at that time. And all because I needed to be able to see my nephew and retrieve some of my brothers belongings from the house, that me and my brother could have as keepsakes. She never gave me or my brother anything. I begged and she kept saying, It's too hard for her to go through his stuff, yet her son was wearing all his clothes. Which was okay, he took him in as his son, as did my family. But why can't we also have some things of my brother? She never let my nephew come over, not once. I barely saw him. It was so hard to go over there, to the place that played such a big part in stealing my brother's life.

But I did, so many times I held back tears, to bring my nephew clothes, shoes and toys from me and his grandpa. I even brought her money for laundry, bought her pads, soap and necessities for herself and the house. And even for her older son. I pleaded with her to come over and bring the boys to swim and spend time together with their cousins so they could grow up together the way my brother would've wanted. She always said they had something else to do and couldn't or she'd say she was on her way and never showed up. She did that several times.

Then, in the midst of all that, on one early afternoon, 5 months after Michael died, I received a video chat from my brother Wayne's grandma. She was in tears, an unbearable sight to see. I said, "grandma, what's wrong?" She said to me that she had received a call from my brother's ex-girlfriend saying that my brother Wayne had been in a motorcycle accident that had claimed his life the day before.

I dropped the phone. This can't be true. His ex-girlfriend is a well-known drug addict, she's high. Why would she say that about my brother? She asked me to look for him, find out and get back to her. Indeed, that's exactly what I was going to do.

But when I got off the phone, I broke down. What if it's true? How will I find my brother? He's homeless so he lives off the grid. I knew a few places where he could be.

I had spoken to him a week prior. He told me he was in another motorcycle accident but he was okay. This boy stayed getting into motorcycle accidents. I remember just feeling concerned, more than usual and I told my brother that I loved him and needed him to be careful out there. He said he would and that he would come to see me soon.

I was in disbelief. I called my baby brother and told him that we needed to find Wayne. Right away my brother goes on his fb page and apparently there were posts up on my brother's page. His friends were talking about the accident and saying Rip to him. Someone made a post that said, "Any family members of Wayne, please contact me" and so I did.

My brother found out where the crash site was but had not found him. I enlisted the help of my cousins. One of which found him. At the coroner's office in Los Angeles. Once again, this is all just a big mistake. And I was going to clear this up and find my brother alive and well, in someone's hospital. And so I started calling hospitals while also calling the coroner's office, they wouldn't answer and no hospitals had him. My cousin said he found him. He was at the coroner's office.

I jumped in my truck and left. If that was him at the coroner's office, he would need to be identified and I wasn't prepared to do this alone. I arrived and I was utterly terrified that I would really be identifying my brother's body. I stood in front of this building on a weekend, hoping they were open. I had driven from Irvine to L.A. This place appears to be closed and I was not about to leave before finding out if that was my brother in there. They had answered the phone for my cousin, someone had to be in there.

After about 30 min I decided to walk to the back of the building. I walked up to some doors and looked through the windows. You could smell the decomposing bodies back there. The smell was strong. My brother can't possibly be back there. The thought was fucking with me. Then someone walked out. Immediately I inquired about seeing if my brother was there. The man said that it shouldn't be a problem. That he would talk to someone and they would let me in.

I waited patiently. I'm on the phone with family trying to give them answers I had not yet had. And then, they let me in. They asked me questions about him. If I was next of kin, etc. And then they let me see him. They wouldn't let me physically see his body, only a picture. And when I looked down, it was him. Laying there, deceased with his eyes open. I touched that picture and looked at my brother in disbelief. I had enough. I walked out of there, unable to hold my composure I screamed and fell to the ground crying and even pissed myself. The hurt I felt was just painful as fuck. We were just coming to grips with my other brother's death and here's another. And with that would be another funeral I had to plan. The 3rd one. Mom, Michael and Wayne. It was a lot for me I admit.

I headed over to the crash site after grabbing my cousin, markers, poster boards and candles to start a vigil. We met up with my baby brother, along with family and friends. Lots of Wayne's friends were there too. They had already got things going. I found out exactly what happened, a car was pulling out of their driveway when my brother and his girl slammed into the car. My brother's motorcycle slid down the street, his girl flew down the street, hitting the grill of a parked car and my brother? Well, he was ejected from his motorcycle and flew into a phone pole down the street, dying instantly.

I saw my baby brother and we just looked at each other at first, as if to silently say to one another, "which one of us is next?" We hugged. We held each other for a while and cried. No one understood our pain.

How could they? We had lost a whole household. Not extended family but an entire household, all intermediate family. People that we looked at every single day. People we ate breakfast lunch and dinner with. People we thought we'd grow old with.

Grandma, grandpa, mom and now our siblings, the closet ones to us. We didn't get the chance to say goodbye. My brother died out there alone. Even though, for some reason, I think Michael was right there. Waiting for his brother. He was his brother's keeper so I know in my heart they are together. On that other side somewhere looking down on us.

Chapter 18

I'm sure we looked okay on the outside, as if we were handling it but inside, we were so broken and confused. That night while lying in my bed going to sleep, I heard a motorcycle pull up outside my bedroom window. It didn't sound like it was from the street, but right at my bedroom window. The engine revved for a minute or so before it took off. The only thing I could think of is that my brother stole someone's bike from the afterlife and came to see his big sister. And why would I expect anything else from him. This boy hadn't learned his lesson, he was still riding around.

I reached out to the mortuary to start the process of getting my brother released from the coroner. Me, my baby brother, his girl and some family went with us to sign paperwork. But then I found out that the coroner had located my brother's dad in prison and that he was legally his next of kin and that he would need to sign paperwork releasing my brother's body to me. If we were to have any kind of funeral. It wasn't easy getting in touch with him either. I had to call the warden up in Wyoming to first notify him that there was a death in the family and to put him in touch with me.

My brother would be held at the coroner's office until further notice. I'm panicking because me and my brother wanted him to have an open casket service just like his big brother. If we didn't get him soon, his body would not be preserved. He needed to be embalmed soon. And then, two days later I received a call from my brother's dad. I had not talked to him in years.

The first thing he said to me was, "Cole, where's my son?" As his voice started cracking. I had to be the one to tell him that his only child, his Jr. was gone. The way that man cried was heart breaking. He pushed through the pain and signed that paperwork, releasing his son to me. We talked for a while. Did some catching up. He asked me if his son was happy before he passed, if he was surrounded by people that loved him, etc. It was a hard phone call.

After that, paperwork was emailed and faxed back and forth from Los Angeles to Wyoming. And within the hour I got a call from the coroners telling me they were getting him ready for transport. And then that night I received a call from the mortuary. WE GOT HIM! And I just cried. It was important that our brother be with us. Just like our mom and other brother. I fought and worked hard for it to happen. I knew they had to be together. And because we were all separated earlier in life, in the end, we all needed to be together, even in death. In the end, all three of those urns needed to be with me.

We, as a family, made his home going amazing. My baby brother and the mother of his children did an amazing job with his suit and the décor. I took care of the financial part, making sure everything was paid for. Family and friends helped out tremendously. I literally had to conduct and direct the funeral myself which was supposed to be done by the mortuary so I was a bit irate. I handled it and we received our due diligence. So after that, everyone headed over to my house where we got drunk and did some night swimming. We had a great night, considering.

Sometimes when I lie in bed at night, I can hear a motorcycle pull up outside my window, I look and never see anything but I know he's there. My lil weewee, coming by to see his big sister. As I'm writing this, it's going on 1 year since Michael passed and 7 months since Wayne. Not a day goes by that I don't think of them or wonder if they made it to mom. And as long as I'm alive I will be wondering what really happened to Michael, as of now, I'm still searching for answers.

Still trying to play an active role in my nephews life, through all my grief. I kept trying and it didn't matter how many times my family reached out to Michael's baby mama to offer some help and try to be a part of their lives, she wouldn't let us. Then one day I had Christmas presents to drop off for the boys and her phone number wasn't working. She always told me I could pop up anytime but I'm just not that type of person. But I was concerned and also needed to get the boys their gifts, so I did. I was there for a while that day, knocking and with no answer, I started to walk away. Then I seen her older son walk up, he let me in the house. My nephew was in there asleep. Me and my boys visited with him. I took pictures of them together and left the presents.

That was the last time I saw my nephew, I received a text a month later from her, saying she moved out. I asked where she was and where my nephew was, she never told me. Asked about my brother's belongings, she said she put them in a storage. So she wasn't upset enough to pack my brother's belongings up and take them somewhere else but she was upset enough to not be able give me and my brother a few things of his. At that point, I had enough of her games and disrespect.

Knowing I couldn't see my nephew or bring him things. Knowing I couldn't have anything to remember my brother by was enough to break me. I decided to stop begging and be at peace with what was happening and because I couldn't change it. She was hurting me and my family and she knew it, she just didn't care. Me and dad had a conversation about wanting to have a healthy relationship with my nephew someday, unfortunately that could be years away when he got old enough to make his own decisions.

As the months went by, I tried to get back to normalcy. I grieved a lot. Other times I kept myself busy. I spent more time with my family. I started to really appreciate the life that was given to me more. But I struggled in areas still. There was a part of me that felt like, God has to have a happy ending for me somewhere. That with all the grief I had endured, that maybe there was someone, somewhere for me that could bring me happiness. After all, I have been single for 7 years now. And it wasn't that I wasn't happy. I was, I mean, my kids made me happy and so did my family. But I felt a little lost and even lonely. I wanted someone to hold me and make me believe everything would be okay. And because I was still scared about what the next day would bring. Would I live the long life I had imagined? Be able to watch my kids grow up, be successful and give me grandbabies that would be sure to keep me young? Would I ever get the chance to get married and experience real love?

And so I prayed for it. I asked God specifically for a God fearing man that loved him more than anything in the world that could make me smile. Then I stopped looking. And decided that God knew what was best and maybe wanted me to wait. And so just the way my life had always unraveled, it continued to do just that, indeed. The devil stayed trying to tear me down, break my spirits. As the kids started a new school year, I'd get a little peace and quiet. Some well needed time alone. But I was facing some difficulties.

While working, I was attacked while getting inside my car, by some man, right here in Irvine. When I opened the door to my vehicle and climbed inside, with the door still open I looked down to get the directions to the address for the delivery I was dropping off. Just then a man appeared out of nowhere, he jumped in my suv, on top of me and tried ripping off my clothes. I fought back, swinging, hitting him over his head several times with this heavy braided ball I had for protection and literally with my feet, I kicked him out of my truck. Slammed the door and took off. We all know I don't like the police and I definitely wasn't about to wait there for them. So I took off almost running him over on the way out.

I had a run in with the police also while grabbing my boys. It wasn't in Irvine this time, but in a neighboring city. I was running late and pulled up to a red curb and attempted to jump out and just grab my boys right quick. They were at the door waiting while two officers happened to be across the street in a vacant parking lot. I didn't see them initially but I heard someone yelling at me from across the street. It was one of the officers yelling at me to move the truck. He was very rude and belligerent towards me.

So while getting back in my truck to move it, I gave him a fucked up look. He should be used to it. I'm not the only person that doesn't like law enforcement. I had nowhere to park so I pulled into the driveway the police were in. Hopped out, grabbed my boys and proceeded back to my vehicle when I saw the officer in the suv pull off. The one on the motorcycle did too. Or so I thought. Normally I would've reversed and probably sped out and luckily I didn't that time. Although no one was in this parking lot, I had put my car in reverse and with my foot still on the brake, something made me look in my rear view camera.

The motorcycle cop was directly behind my truck. He wasn't writing me a ticket. He was simply sitting there with his torso turned toward my truck so his body cam would catch everything. It startled the fuck out of me. My boys were panicking wanting to know what was happening. I didn't even know what was happening. I just knew that I was sitting there with my truck's reverse lights on and this officer was not moving.

It suddenly dawned on me what was happening. He wanted me to back up into him so he could arrest me for assault on an officer with a deadly weapon or so he could have a reason to shoot up my truck because technically my truck is a deadly weapon. This officer saw me put my boys in the truck, he was fully aware there were kids in this truck and he didn't care. His redneck ass saw my mixed kids and decided to fuck with me. I went live on Facebook and recorded the whole thing, while my friends pleaded with me to put the truck in park and turn it off. I did. The officer pulled off but he didn't leave. He pulled on the sidewalk just at the parking lot exit.

I handed my son the phone and had him crouch down and extended his arm to keep recording while I pulled out. I had my youngest crouch down as well. I didn't know if this officer was going to shoot us. He didn't and we got on. But I'd continue seeing him everywhere, every time I was in Santa Ana dropping or picking up my boys. I'd spot him behind other cars at stop lights, staring at me, waiting for me to fuck up. I did what I had to and got my kids out of there and into another after school program and area entirely.

After working so hard to find answers about my brother Michael's death, I finally got the toxicology and autopsy reports and even video footage of my brothers last moments on that stairwell. I wanted so badly to believe that someone took my brother from me, truth is, he sat down, lit up a foil pipe, smoked that meth/fentanyl and fell over. His last conscious moments were in that dark stairwell alone. And it fucked me up inside. I'm currently awaiting my other brother Wayne's autopsy and toxicology reports. I never thought to get his because we knew what happened but I suppose I'd like to know what he ate that day. What drugs were in his system, if he had any pre-existing health problems, etc.

As a safety precaution I went on to make sure I was completely healthy myself, only to find out I had stage 1 melanoma cancer in two places, after letting my dermatologist cut away at me, I am cancer free. Two more scars, serving a constant reminder that for whatever reason, God isn't finished with me yet. They say only the strongest survive and I have every intention of doing just that.

Life is an interesting journey, you never know where you'll end up. With good, always comes the bad. It seems as if I'm always left wondering, what's next? And because there's always some drama unfolding somewhere. When I look back on my life I see struggle & triumph. I see very weak moments that lead to my strengths. I see why I had to go through so much to get this level. Sometimes on the way to the top, you'll experience shit that may make you think "this is the worst time of my life." But at the end of it, through all the adversity, if you can get to where you wanted to be, you begin to understand that whatever don't kill you, indeed makes you stronger.

We all have our stories, our battles. When I first started this book it was because of my grief. I came to the realization that life is so very short. As I wrote and wrote, I continued to lose people around me. Including a dear friend of mine that promised me he'd direct the movie for this book and it would be a big accomplishment for us both. I have no doubt that my Ace would've made that happen. In this book God allowed me to revisit the places in life where I experienced grief and humiliation over and over to remind me of where I came from. I don't know what kind of time I'm looking at but this is me signing my name in the cement before it dries. I don't want to leave this earth as a nobody. I keep finding the momentum I need to keep rising to the top, but I often wonder, how do I get my life back when I get there? I came, I saw and I conquered. I am Stormy!

Phone rings

Mutual friend: "Chaos is on his way out Nik and he's looking for you!!"

Phone drops

...To be continued...

www.ingramcontent.com/pod-product-compliance
Lightning Source LLC
Chambersburg PA
CBHW050636160426
43194CB00010B/1698